"Mary Mad takes care to address the d[...] college student faces in this beautiful re[...] Within those difficulties, she shares how God has met her, led her, and [...] ly taught her faithfully through each season. If you're looking to encourage a college student, this book will be a gift."

   - **Brenna Blain**, Christian speaker and host of the podcast "Can I Say That?"

"Throughout this book, Mary Mad consistently points college students away from isolation and into a place to belong: the local church. I'm thankful for books like this that remind us of the value of living in the light. I would recommend this book to any college student who wants God to be at the center of their college experience."

   - **Cole Shiflet**, Executive Director of Anchored Passion & Multiply Groups

"Get out your highlighters and pens because you'll want to take notes. MMS is a brilliant wordsmith whose writing is relatable, inspiring, and comforting. Whether preparing for college, currently in college, never attended college, or a post-college graduate—I really believe this book offers wisdom and insight for all readers. I was both challenged and encouraged while reading through *Contemplations of a Collegiate Christian*. I imagine it will sit on my bookshelf for many years to come as I recommend it to guests of my home and pick it up for wisdom from time to time. I am thankful this book exists."

   - **Madison Weeks**, creator of the *Me Too, Sister* Ministry

contemplations *of a* collegiate christian

THOUGHTS ON FORGOING THE WORLD AND CLINGING
TO CHRIST IN YOUNG ADULTHOOD

m.m. schumpert

UNITED HOUSE

Scripture marked (NLT) are taken from the Holy Bible, New Living Translation, copyright © 1996, 2004, 2015 by Tyndale House Foundation. Used by permission of Tyndale House Publishers, Inc., Carol Stream, Illinois 60188. All rights reserved.

Scriptures marked (ESV) are from The ESV® Bible (The Holy Bible, English Standard Version®), copyright © 2001 by Crossway, a publishing ministry of Good News Publishers. Used by permission. All rights reserved.

Scriptures marked (NIV) are from THE HOLY BIBLE, NEW INTERNATIONAL VERSION® NIV® Copyright © 1973, 1978, 1984 by International Bible Society® Used by permission. All rights reserved worldwide.

ISBN: 978-1-952840-17-3

UNITED HOUSE Publishing
Waterford, Michigan
info@unitedhousepublishing.com
www.unitedhousepublishing.com

Interior design: Matt Russell, Marketing Image, mrussell@marketing-image.com

Printed in the United States of America
2022—First Edition

SPECIAL SALES
Most UNITED HOUSE books are available at special quantity discounts when purchased in bulk by corporations, organizations, and special-interest groups. For information, please e-mail orders@ unitedhousepublishing.com.

Dedicated to every Christian college student
who thought they were alone in their struggles,
who was too afraid to put words to their fears,
who couldn't find language for their hurts and joys,
who longs to know Christ more and make Him known.

And to the Greenhouse:
We learned many of these lessons together;
I just happen to be the one writing them down.

And to Kyle Schumpert,
my number one fan,
my biggest counselor,
my constant,
the love of my life.

if you get nothing else out of this book

My utmost desire for these words is this: may they glorify God, not the college experience. God changes the college experience, not vice versa. So, if I emphasize that truth in this book, may He be praised. If I do not, please forgive me, and try to forget any wrong idea this book might embed in your head.

It's difficult to find the balance between writing all the beautiful intricacies of the collegiate adventure while also making sure each one is attributed to its appropriate Author, the Lord. I don't want to be redundant in my statements, but if that's what it takes for you to not miss this vital point (that only God deserves our undivided love) then redundancy is necessary.

So, before we move on into the stories, giggles, and lessons learned, allow me to say this:

I want you to finish this book, set it down, and desire God, not simply desire college. Seek Him, know Him—not the college experience. Seek Him now, wherever you are. If you are in college, this will likely be more helpful to you, but if you're not, joy is just as available. Keep chanting this to yourself, praying it becomes more true as I have:

Jesus changes everything.

Jesus, somehow, someway, is the answer to whatever you are struggling with right now. Jesus is the answer to your yearning spirit. He's the answer to your aching for purpose. He's the answer to true "success." He's the answer to your grief. He's the answer to your confusion. He's the answer to your broken friendships. He's the answer to your longing for significance. He's the answer to freedom from your addictions. He's the answer to your desire to be truly known and truly loved. He's even the answer to your boredom. He's the answer to your discontented singleness or marriage. He's the answer to your numbness, depression, or anxiety.* He's the answer to getting your "best four years" while you are in college.

Don't be deceived—this doesn't mean knowing Him comes easy. Knowing Him takes time, wrestling, helpful community, deep study of the Word, and heaps of prayer. But somehow, in all the seeking, He will show up. He will change everything for the better when we ask Him, including the four years of college.

Put Jesus at the center, and you will get something you couldn't have imagined for yourself. Enthrone and crown Him King of your life, and He will make joy spew from your soul. Desire Him, and you will get more than you could ever desire.

That's all this book is really about. I just finished up my time as a college student, and I've watched God move in mighty ways. I've also messed up and had idols fall before my eyes. I want to specifically talk to college students about these things. But for all the words written, the topics covered, specific examples explained, and stories told, the lesson of this book is actually pretty simple:

Jesus changes everything.

If nothing else, I pray you find this true. Please don't remember my name; just remember Christ. Don't even bother with remembering the title of this book; just remember the aching in your heart for Him to be the center of your everything, and use that to fuel your time in college.

Chase Him down with all that you are, and then watch as He changes your mourning into song, your sadness into gladness, your doubt into assurance, your death into life.

This is what I want you to get out of this book.

As a person who has struggled through a difficult season of this myself, I want to note this is not to say that medication or counseling is not helpful. It is, and Jesus will use it to bring healing. He is the answer, and yes, He often uses the raw materials of this world to heal and renew humans.

table of contents

introduction:
time to be honest

"To love at all is to be vulnerable"
C.S. Lewis

Honest words are my "love language," if you will. I love it when people say things that are so relatable and raw it makes me want to get on my knees and beg them to say more. I love it when someone translates exactly what my heart has been trying to process. I love the small phrases or verses that feel so big and real you want to share them with everyone you know, to tattoo them all over your body, and write them on your bedroom walls.

The truest form of honesty stands hand-in-hand with vulnerability. Vulnerability is priceless and beautiful. It's raw and messy, and it stings in all the little places you didn't know existed, but it's a beautiful type of hurt; the type that ignites healing. It's like the burn of hydrogen peroxide cleaning something you didn't even know was infected. My husband Kyle and I were just talking the other day about how honest vulnerability, no matter how scary, always seems to be the key to breakthroughs in every sense. No matter the season, or the relationship, the pattern seems to go like this: honesty and vulnerability breakdown strongholds and spark breakthroughs.

David talks about this pattern of renewal in Psalm 66:18-20 (ESV):

"If I had not confessed the sin in my heart,
the Lord would not have listened.
But God did listen!
He paid attention to my prayer.

contemplations of a collegiate christian

Blessed be God,
because he has not rejected my prayer
or removed his steadfast love from me!"

David's honesty about his sin leads to a breakthrough of renewed intimacy with *Yahweh*. This makes sense because God loves and honors honesty in all forms, especially in the deepest parts of our hearts (Psalm 51:6). He loves it when we don't act like we have it all together. He loves it when we admit our faults and weaknesses, ask Him for wisdom and guidance, and when we ask Him to do the thing only He can do: to make us like Him.

So, honesty can definitely reference the hard stuff, like our sins and griefs, but it doesn't always. Other times, things are hard to admit simply because they are so wonderful, and they expose our sensitivity to beauty. Beauty exposes our humanness, our moveableness, our smallness, our soul-ness. It's like when you see a sunset and can't help but scream out to everyone around to "LOOK!!!" Or when you are so moved by a song because it cuts you so beautifully, but it seems so silly how affected you are, so you don't admit to anyone how much you really love it. Instead, you look it up on Spotify and add it to your secret playlist.* But if you were just honest about it, by expressing your sensitivity to beauty, you would be able to experience it in an even deeper way, with people awe-struck alongside you. Honesty would change your experience of the magical secret Spotify song into a communal, awe-inspiring affair.

My grandfather once traveled to the Grand Canyon alone. He recounted the deep red valleys as the most beautiful things he'd ever seen, but he recalled being sad he had gone alone. He longed for someone to gasp at the landscape alongside him.

Celebration and grief are both meant to be shared. Honesty about both the hard and the beautiful requires vulnerability. And vulnerability, when met with love and truth, changes things for the better.

I know that I could always use a little bit more of this pattern of honesty and vulnerability, and so I thought I might write this book, and in it, try to be honest

---

* *This happened to me in Frozen 2, no joke. I got choked up in the movie theater, but I was so embarrassed about how affected I was over a children's movie that I didn't tell anyone that I cried until hours later.*

introduction: time to be honest

about a season that has a decade worth of hard and beautiful things all packed into a few short years—college.

College has been the most fruitful and terrifying season of my life. God has used it to rip me apart and piece me back together, and I think it's worth sitting down and discussing with a bit of candor. I believe it will be beneficial to hash out all of the common struggles and celebrations of the season. I want to get specific about the vital things like choosing careers, dating, anxiety, making friends, and the nearly-celestial experience of morning coffee and time with God. I want to use my experiences, God's Word, and the wisdom I've gathered from some godly voices in my life to shape both of our perspectives of this season. I hope we come out the other side of these pages with a fearless excitement about what God can do here in this transformative time. He is able to make these years absolutely joyful when we are willing to submit to His kingship.

I hope you find this book to be sweetly honest, refreshing, and healing. I hope you feel free to consider fears that you didn't realize you had, and I want you to please know you aren't alone in your fears of adulthood. There are a million others who are walking through this season with the same questions and concerns.

But most importantly, what we all need to know is we are not alone because our God is walking with us. None of this is a mistake; He is above all experiences and seasons—He knows us, and He understands us. And if we tune our ears to listen, He will speak timeless truths into this time-bound season—truths that will calm our hearts and energize our souls to take on our collegiate time with fewer fears and more faith.

I pray the Lord calls to you through these pages, invites you to step out of fear and into an abundant, Holy Spirit-saturated life, showing you He can make water flow from dry ground. He wants you to know Him, to know victory in Him, and celebrate all that is wonderful about this season in which He has placed you.

You won't find any new ideas in this book because I'm not that original. This book is just a record of my thoughts as a twenty-first-century Christian college student. I'm simply wrestling through what the Gospel means and how it has changed my college life, just like you are. All I aim to do in these pages is take any worries, cares, and fears and focus them around these realities: God is our loving Father, Jesus is better than anything, and the Holy Spirit is within us. These three realities have changed everything for me. I live my most abundant days—the life Jesus has called me to—when I talk about them, so I want to invite you into this adventure of peering into these realities.

I'll give suggestions on how we could do and think about this season better in light of these realities. We are called to follow Jesus, so what does that look like in the context of college and job searching and becoming independent? What does "success" look like to Jesus, and how has it been misrepresented in the world and in our churches? How would He do college? How does Jesus change the way we think about our jobs, roommates, free time, money, and education? How would He search for a job? What would His friendships look like? What is God ultimately calling us to in this season? I hope we can get a clearer picture together.

I don't claim to be an expert. By the time I finish this book, I will have only graduated college for a few months, but I think that's kind of the point; you know? I want to let God enter in *this* moment and *this* season while it's happening. I want us to trust Him in this current moment, not just in post-college, looking back, after the season has passed. I want Him in the here and now.

This isn't a book of wisdom for you to strictly follow, so test everything you read here against the Word and use discernment. I'm just offering some thoughts and considerations for young Christians in the twenty-first-century context, while I wrestle with them myself. I don't expect you to think anything here is ground-breaking, but I want to offer the space and language to talk about your specific college worries and cares. I want the floor to be open for discussion, and I hope you walk away from this book re-thinking something you hadn't considered before, asking Jesus to enter into a part of your college life or young adulthood you hadn't invited Him into before. I hope His eternal promises change your temporary perspective.

For those of you who haven't been this young in a while, you are welcome to these pages too! But, if you begin to think these worries and cares are silly, that such fears are immature, I ask you to take a step back for a moment. Remember those long study sessions, stinging words of romantic rejection, the consistent fear of missing out, career and major-choosing, and the newness of adult anxieties. Those were serious worries and anxieties. Consider with compassion that we are growing up in a world much different than your own, one full of dis-

introduction: time to be honest

traction, endless options, social pressure, and political tension. Remember how Jesus commands us to bring all of our cares, big and small fears, kindergarten and college fears, young adult and elderly fears to Him. Bring them *all*. So don't discount your former young self, and don't discount the worries of those who are just becoming adults now. Instead, empathize with our fears, and offer solutions and encouragement as we learn to live out the Gospel as young adults. I believe this will serve all of us best.

So here I am, laying all of it down on these pages. Here are my confessions and contemplations, fears of failure, and recountings of grace. Here's to college and young adulthood—the highs and the lows, the fears and the thrills, the falling apart as He pieces us back together, more beautifully than we could ever imagine.

Here are the contemplations of a collegiate Christian.

ONE

the hardest four years

"We are not necessarily doubting that God will do the best for us;
we are wondering how painful that best will turn out to be."

C.S. Lewis

All I knew about college before I arrived was that everyone said it was "the best four years of your life," and so that's what I was expecting when I arrived on campus.

In some ways, this has been very true for me. I've absolutely loved my time here. I've gained deep and true friendships, learned so much about God's design of the world through my classes*, lived on my own and made my own decisions, and still indulged with late-night chats, too much coffee, last-minute road trips, and silly laughter and flirting. Everything in college was a little bit more sparkly than it was in high school, and I was more free than ever before to do as I pleased. Possibilities for adventure seemed endless. Potential felt like it was constantly leaking out of the campus grounds and into my blood. Maybe I'm a romantic, but I often felt like the star in the opening of a musical, tap dancing as I was high on life.

University life can be absolutely invigorating and liberating, and I wouldn't trade my university experience for anything—not even for a four-year tour of the entire globe. I mean that deep in my core, down in my bone marrow—this season has been that valuable, precious, and transformative. However, I'm still not sure that "the best four years" is quite the way I would summarize college.

---

* I did not attend a Christian university. My university was secular, but I made so many connections about God's creative design by looking at Scripture and seeing how it lined up with my studies.

contemplations of a collegiate christian

That's a simple statement, and it's more complex than that.

There are two sides to every coin, so the complex part is that college has been both the best season and the hardest season so far. Beauty involves pain, and consequently, the most beautiful seasons often erupt out of the most excruciating ones. The excitement, chaos, adventure, and thrill have also been accompanied by confusion, fear, and anxiety unlike ever before.

The experiences seem to come in couplets: the scariest and most encouraging era, the most fun and most serious moments, the most potential to succeed and the most to fail, the most exciting and the most discouraging, the best and the hardest years of my life so far.

This newfound collegiate freedom made all of my fears more raw and real than they were in high school; they seemed more pressing and intense. Since amplified freedom also meant amplified responsibility, there were times when I felt far too small for the task, so much that it made me tremble and weep.

The new context of young adulthood drew out all of my questions, baggage, brokenness, fearful hopes, and illusions of what it means to be a "grown-up." I often felt torn apart by confusion, misunderstanding, and frustration, resulting in dark and scary moments, some of the most fearful times of my life.

But there is one person who made all the difference in my college life. He called my darkness to light, my fears to hope, and what often felt like death to a newness of life:

God, my kind and loving and patient Father.

He used my specific anxieties, risky decisions, immaturity, aimless class schedule, blind passions, underdeveloped skills, and zeal for the Gospel to call me into a new season of hope, life, love, excitement, sacrifice, and the best years of my life so far.

He caused something beautiful to erupt out of my few short years here, using college as a gracious undoing, a sweet dissolving, a steep slope in sanctification.

I've spent hours in prayer, seeking wisdom from a Father who I felt had forgotten me at times, and it was hard. But He never did, and He was using each moment to draw me nearer, to make this era all that it has been—such a beautiful time. Because of the hard, I know Him better now than I did before, and *that* is what made these the best, most beautiful four years so far.

Like beauty and pain, best and hard can go together. God uses hard and turns it into a vessel for His glory. He uses our weaknesses to show us His strength, giving us joy in the Gospel. Our best at college might be massively different than we want it to be, but that just goes to show that the common factor in our best years is always this: *being saturated in Jesus.*

Our best years aren't childhood or college. They aren't necessarily adulthood either. They're not our most "free" years. No, they're the years when we know Jesus the most, when we hold onto Him like the treasure that He truly is and when He fills us with joy He has promised. Those are our best years.

So latch on to this truth, readers:

Beauty and pain, best and hard can co-exist.

Because no matter the season or situation, *He* is our source of joy, our best years.

So when I graduate, and when someone asks me about college, or when I give advice to a teenager who is about to head to a big adventure at their university, I will want to say this:

According to my experience, it will be the best, and it will be the hardest time of your life. Brace yourself, and get excited for possibly the greatest adventure of your lifetime, up to this point. You are about to be challenged like never before. You are about to be undone and reformed in ways you never thought were attainable. You are going to have a billion options and possibilities thrown at you. But no matter what—I beg of you—please don't forget Jesus. Don't take your eyes off of Him. Don't get your heart set on a specific type of "success" that excludes His standard. Don't get so caught up in the world that you forget who created it. Be quick to ask for His wisdom. Expect that God will change your dreams and hopes into something new at times and willingly let Him do it. Trust Him, even when the change hurts and you're afraid. He's good, and He only changes bad things into good things, good things into better things, even when you can't imagine it getting any better.

It will take faith to walk through the season and see the other side. When fear and hurt do come your way, and you don't know where He is, wrestle *with* Him through your fears like Jacob did (Genesis 32:22-32), and He will wrestle with you patiently and kindly, though ever so severely when necessary. You might be changed from the inside out, ripped to pieces and shattered, but don't despise your Father's discipline because He won't waste a moment of pain, and He promises it will end in blessing (Hebrews 12:5). It's only for your good. You might even walk away limping like Jacob, but I promise you this: if He's the One who's changing you, the One you wrestle with, the One you submit to, it will be absolutely beautiful. Eternally worth it.

Because just when you think you're too broken, too far gone, too overwhelmed by it all, too weak and confused, He will call out to you and piece your life back together more beautifully than you ever could conceive it—to His glory.

These might be the hardest years, up to this point.

These might be the best years, up to this point.

The choice is yours:

Will you forget Him, walk away from Him, ignore His calls, resist Him, and run from Him?

Or, even when it's scary, will you seek Him, wrestle with Him, trust Him, and surrender to such a gracious undoing?

TWO

what is success?

"If there were a choice—and he suspected there was—a choice between, on the one hand, the heights and the depths and, on the other hand, some sort of safe, cautious middle way, he, for one, here and now chose the heights and the depths."

Sheldon Vanauken, A *Severe Mercy*

"Success" is a vague term the world throws around a lot.

"We just want you to be successful."

"I want to set my children up for success."

"She has been such a successful person!"

But when the term is never intentionally explained, we naturally fill in the gaps with our own definition. From a young age, I gathered that success meant making a lot of money (hopefully at something you enjoy, but mostly a lot of money), being well-educated and well-behaved, following a moral life sprinkled with Jesus, having a beautiful home, being married with children, and growing old with a good retirement saved so I could watch my children and grandchildren do the same thing.

To the fault of no one in particular, this was the definition of success I formulated over my lifetime.

When I graduated high school and went off to college, I was on a mission to achieve this more "successful" version of myself. I expected college would be the best four years of my life because I would go to a fancy liberal arts school where I found my best friends all in one sorority. I would have the time of my life but also be well-behaved and on fire for Jesus. I would end up in the medical field or in law school, which I would often utilize for evangelistic purposes, right after I traveled the world for a bit doing adventurous, but still resume-building things. Finally, I would settle down and get married after I was financially stable and ready to raise well-behaved children, and thus, start the cycle all over again for another generation.

That was the plan, formed from my definition of success. While I hadn't written my ten-year plan down on paper, I also hadn't allowed Jesus to write out my definition of a life well-lived, and the world took the front seat and etched a plan into my imagination, my future hopes, and my heart. The world was driving the car of my ambitions, and Jesus was in the back seat, asking me to let Him upfront. Somewhere after my conversion in eighth grade and before my senior year in high school, I lost sight of the type of self-sacrificing life Jesus was calling me to and replaced it with a more comfortable, socially acceptable, people-pleasing version. I compromised without realizing what was happening.

As you might have guessed, He shook my sleeping soul awake, inviting me into success more beautiful than I could ever have imagined. Through His gracious kindness and discipline, He completely wrecked my original plan.

My agenda was off track before college even began, when I came, kicking and screaming, to my public university. I would have rather been *anywhere* but my home state of Mississippi. I wanted to be at *any* liberal arts college that worshiped academics rather than an SEC school that worshiped football. I did not think my goals of prestige and adventure were waiting for me here in the deep South, the land of fried chicken and white Jesus. I wanted to get *out*, and I was convinced that my highlight-reel life was waiting for me far beyond the Mason Dixon line. Yet, my finances were telling me otherwise, so here I was, stuck in Mississippi.

Once I got settled on my campus, I ended up deciding (like millions of other college students) that medical school, engineering, and law school actually weren't my callings.[*] I spent a couple of years and many semesters crying about my career choices, seeking something else that was prestigious and socially respectable, knowing anything with a hefty salary was probably not what God was calling me to but being afraid of losing the stability and respect I so desired. I wanted to feel respected by societal standards, and I so desired financial security I would weep sometimes, desperate for God to give me the "go" on medical school or something besides writing. I was clawing to get worldly approval, yet I felt God tugging me in another direction, always away from the respect and admiration I craved.

Instead of graduating college to lead a single travel-savvy life, collecting wild experiences and exotic memories like I thought, I ended up falling in love with, dating, and marrying the man who I swore would "never find himself a girl-friend, and much less a WIFE!" (Quote by me. True story.)

All this happened before I graduated college.

Only about two years in, you could say, my ten-year plan didn't really work out, and yet I couldn't be more grateful to God for wrecking my original plans. Eventually, He woke me up to the truth of the matter: life is either lived for His glory or mine. It's either lived for His approval or others'. There's no portion I can withhold from Him; it's all or nothing with Christ. The Holy Spirit reminded me that a heart divided between the world and Him isn't a commitment; it's spiritual adultery. True freedom can't be found when we are divided and adulterous in regards to Christ. We must be fully committed, fully married to the only One who can offer us satisfaction, or we will feel the division deep in our souls, tearing us apart. That's what was happening to me; I was being torn by my own desire for worldly gain.

So I repented of my compromising, and along the way, He redefined success for me. His version of "success" looks much different than the world, and I had mixed the two definitions somewhere along the way.

He was calling me to give up everything that would make me seem respectable to many in my American, money-driven, prestige-obsessed context, in an even deeper sense than I had previously thought, let go of it all to follow Him. He was calling me—as He calls all of us—to give up the world for the purpose of

---

* By the way...can we please work on telling our children how many different careers there are? Can we tell them about all of the possibilities, instead of focusing on like five jobs we have all decided are the best? We don't all have to look the same. I think it'd be helpful for all of us if we worked on this a little. Those of us who aren't made to be in one of those few golden careers would spend more time dreaming and working towards the things God made us for.

gaining my soul.* Following Him would become the measure of my success.

After this redefining, I started to align my life to His definition, and I could never have imagined being so content and joyful in the season in which God has placed me, despite all my frustration along the way. The same God that called me to my SEC school, beckoned me from medicine to writing, led me to my sweet husband-the love of my life, Kyle Schumpert, to our sweet and simple adventure of sacrificial marital love. He taught me to chase His will above my own.

So what is His definition of success? Getting married early and writing a book? Changing careers? Is this the key?

No, it's not. Neither marital nor career status are involved. The success I found is exclusive from any sort of awards I'd won. It doesn't have anything to do with my finances. It's independent of any world traveling or book writing. My story of "success" is not reliant on these things; they are just facets of my story.

Single or married, rich or poor, well-educated or dumb-as-a-rock—these things aren't the standard. These cannot be the criteria of "success" for a Christian, and we really underestimate, cheat, and rob our life's goal of what it's really worth when we measure it by these standards. Though we often run after awards, high GPAs, ambitious internships, exotic study abroad trips, and romance, these are fading and feeble attempts at true success. They are not the soul-freeing success that is available to Christians.

So what is it? You're getting impatient. I'm taking a long time; I know. I just wanted to take a moment to really make sure this point was impressed in your mind:

Success doesn't tangibly play out the same way for everyone.

Here it is: The "success" I discovered is worth so much more than those small representations. It's more simple, refreshing, and attainable than any of those surface-level things. It is actually very ordinary and accessible, yet it's mourn-

---

* *"And what do you benefit if you gain the whole world but lose your own soul? Is anything worth more than your soul?" (Matthew 16:26, NLT).*

what is success?

fully rare.

I hold a strong belief that only defining life by an image-obsessed, resume-building standard is limiting and heart-breakingly empty. That standard will leave us slaves to our resumes, experiences, and highlight-reel moments, which—God's Word has promised us—will all fade and die with time.

I have learned that relationship status, financial outcome, graduate school acceptance, cool traveling plans, or anything else we like to name as a marker of success and "making the most of your twenties" will come up short and hauntingly hollow without the simple, ordinary, Gospel-invading and marinating everyday lives.

Through all the disappointments, the tears, the struggling for something God wasn't offering me, I learned what "success" really means: *living out the Gospel, right here and right now, in whatever way possible, with the resources He has given me, in the context of where He has placed me.*

The simple Gospel—that God gave His life for human sinners, giving them His own Spirit, making them saints and co-heirs of Christ—is extraordinary in its implications for young adults.

The Gospel turned lonely singleness into a unique position to give myself fully to the world of an eternal kingdom.

In the same way, it turned the daunting idea of marriage into an opportunity to be sanctified, in the most intimate way, hand-in-hand with another believer.

The Gospel took my fears of never being respected or financially stable and wrote them into prayers of surrender to God's design for my brain and career.

The Gospel changed my desire to live a more adventurous, world-traveling life into a desire to minister to the world right outside my front door, in whatever way that manifests in my present season.

The Gospel turns my boring 9-to-5 days into a spiritual mission field.

The Gospel has changed those I once only considered my acquaintances, co-workers, and lab partners into the Church—the truest and best family.

contemplations of a collegiate christian

The Gospel takes my longing for a big salary and turns it into a longing to invest in something eternal.

The Gospel takes this sinful, confused, faltering young Mary Mad and calls her a saint, calls her to live more abundantly and joyfully than she could ever imagine.

The Gospel has turned all of my cookie-cutter, empty, American ideas of life—and even my hippie, unconventional-life dreams—and flipped them into an eternal desire to proclaim Christ resurrected.

The Gospel has changed every thought I had about what success was and wasn't and turned them upside down: His glory in exchange for my own.

It's funny, isn't it? Jesus is the most "successful" person of all if you really think about it because He fully embodied the Gospel. He is the Gospel. He is God. Jesus is *God*, and He could have been a doctor, a lawyer, rich, famous, good-looking, had a family with 3.2 well-behaved kids, yet He didn't do this. He held the title of a simple carpenter boy from small-town Nazareth, and He was not handsome at all (Isaiah 53:2). He had a blue-collar job, and He lived a disrespected, persecuted, homeless, poor, and single life. However, He used every resource for the Father's will, living perfectly in step with it and in perfect submission to His lot on Earth, and He said we should follow His example into eternal life.

And yet, we wave our Christian flags, all the while, saying, "You can live that life of submission to God's will and design for you, Jesus! That's awesome for you! But I actually really have it a little more figured out over here; I know I don't really have these skills, and you haven't called me to this career, but the salary seems fitting, right? And I know that they aren't supposed to be my spouse, but we would make beautiful babies; am I right? I'm the exception to the rule of joy you've laid out. I found life another way. But you're still my Savior and Lord! No tension between us! We're good!"

He is the definition of what it means to be fulfilled, joyful, and perfect, and truly "successful," and yet, many college students don't *really listen* to Him when it comes to planning and dreaming out our lives. Even if we act as we do, the conversation usually mimics the one above.

what is success?

Make Him the *center*. Crown Him your *King*. Let your college life rotate around *Him*…

This will change everything in the most life-giving way possible.

Actually, you won't find life any other way (John 14:6).

That said, I must emphasize once again that the Gospel is uniquely individual in its implications. Since God calls individuals to live out the Gospel, your twenties will not necessarily play out the same as mine or Jesus' because you are an *individual*, distinct from any other person. You might not have five room-mates, choose to get married, or end up writing a book about it all. Your time-line and your events *will* look different than mine because we are not the same person. You might be married during college, or you might be headed to the mission field as a single person. You might have a highly-valued career and use it to serve the kingdom, or you might be headed to an adventure of stay-at-home motherhood. You might start a homeless ministry one day. You might be a teacher at a low-income school and love your students' families well. You might become a garbage man who uses his days to pray and get to know his neighbors.

This kind of success is in the heart attitude, not in the blueprint. So, no matter what the occupation or life plan is on the surface, as a Christian, the core of our success is the same: God's love is magnified through our days as we treasure Him in our hearts. What decisions make Him more precious to you? That's the definition of your success.

Christ is magnified—this is the Christian's definition of success, in college or not.

No degree could ever compare to discipleship under Christ.

No future salary could ever overcome the richness of provision.

No social-media-perfect romance holds a candle to intimacy with the Trinity.

No cool international travels to far-off kingdoms will outlast the adventure of serving with the true King in the sweat-and-blood construction of His everlasting Kingdom, in the here and now.

contemplations of a collegiate christian

No graduate program could quench our longing for the truest scholarship, that bittersweet lesson called grace.

This is the kind of success that lasts.

This type of success lifts my eyes from my resumé to His face.

This is the kind of success I've been yearning for all along.
And all these things and more are ours in Christ, who has rescued us from worldly success and called us into something more eternal and lasting.

I now know joy is not found in living out the ideal Pinterest or Instagram-worthy life. It's found in a person and God named Jesus. And my disappointment of not reaching the previous "success" I wanted was the place where He showed up so evidently, giving a more "successful" life than I could imagine.

For our weaknesses in our exams, for our anxieties about fifth-years, for our daily distresses about relationships, and for our endless failures, His strength fills all our chasms, bridges all of our shortcomings (1 Corinthians 12:9-11).

If I only trust Him and take Him at His Word, all my fears and failures can be created into a marvelous cascade of worship. An altar of praise where I let go of all that I want to be and trade it in for all that He is, exchanging anxiety, control, and endless chasing for peace, trust, and satisfaction.

I'm learning to trust in Him and His success. I'm learning to stop replacing the Gospel with fading and empty ideas of what it means to "make the most of my twenties" or live my "best four years."

With this new lesson of what abundant life actually means, I have a deep suspicion that "the best four years" is going to become a trend extending beyond my twenties, invading my thirties, forties, and the decades to follow. Because as I believe Him more than the culture around me, choosing His voice over the empty traps thrown my way, He will show up. And where He is, abundant life is.

I pray this book helps you picture what success could mean for you through the Gospel, dear reader. I pray the crosses you bear become your joy, as you seek Jesus. Proclaim His kingship in this season, and you will find He will fill it with joy beyond measure. Ask the Holy Spirit to invade your lecture halls, dorm rooms, body, daily habits, thoughts, study sessions, 8:00 ams, part-time jobs, desires, prayers, search for truth, speech, financial decisions, internships, friendships, singleness, dating, wedding-planning, coffee dates, microwaved meals, late nights, early mornings, moments of deep lament and moments of heart-trilling joy. Do this, and it will radically transform your soul and your life.

Only trust Him, seek Him, follow Him, and He will be faithful to fill those moments with life beyond measure.

As He becomes greater and we become lesser, our best days are now and forever. This scary season can be a sweet slope leading to an adventure of knowing Christ more deeply than ever.

This is an invitation—to both of us—to re-think what it means to do college (and beyond) with Christ at the center.

I graduated with a deep sense of gratitude, a large dose of humility, and a better, more "successful" college-era that I never could have imagined on my own, simply because Christ became bigger, and I became smaller. I got a better deal than I was bargaining for because God reformed my idea of "success" along the way. I long to define success this way for the rest of my life.

I hope you find, as I have, collegiate Christianity actually has far less to do with avoiding alcohol, practicing abstinence, getting a good salary, and finding the perfect spouse, and a lot more to do with getting intimate with mercy, getting your hands covered in grace, and holding fast to Him every step along the way. If you replace the latter with the former, you just might find yourself far from the joy that Christ promises us—which is, after all, Himself—grace, mercy, and ultimate "success" embodied.

THREE

trading in selfish years

"Joy is the serious business of heaven"
C.S. Lewis

It's a common statement that college years are the "selfish years." Before full-blown adulthood starts, before marriage, before all the grown up responsibilities hit hard causing us to yearn for naptime and recess again, these precious years are the prime time to experiment and indulge all of our selfish desires.

I've always held a particular suspicion of this statement, and recently, I resolved that no matter how well-intended the phrase is, it just can't be true for believers.

No matter how tempting it is to believe these years are mine to claim, to experiment, to treat myself, to collect experiences, to focus on me-time, to indulge just for the heck of it, this can't be a Christian practice, even if it *sounds* really fun.

This is simply because Jesus says that's not how it works.

He said if we lose our lives, deny ourselves, sacrifice our flesh at the altar of our lives, we get more of Him. And *He* is the way to true life.

And since the only way to life is through Him, and in order to get to Him, we must deny ourselves (Matthew 16:24-2), selfish years don't seem to be an option.

So for those of us who are following Jesus, these are not our selfish years. We actually have no time for selfish years, friends! God's kingdom is heading our way quickly, and our greatest joy is in Christ, more of Him and less of us—can I get an amen? Even better, we have no need for selfishness; we actually get something so much better, so much more satisfying than selfishness.

We get selfless servitude.

I know, I know. That doesn't initially sound enticing, and I admit; I used to cringe at that word too, but I think it's because we have been taught to. We think selfish years mean plane tickets, more "treating yo self," cool outfits, midnight fun dancing and romance, independence, a sense of freedom, bright colors, and *Mamma Mia*-like experiences. And as for servitude, we think that means stiff-necked, nun-like, no-fun, rule-following behavior. No time for funny business or excitement; we are strictly here to serve like machines, like soldiers, marching in the Lord's army, literally washing people's feet, denying our existence and our need for rest, starving ourselves and eating a diet of stale crackers and vegetable broth (when we aren't fasting, of course). Lots of stiff outfits, stinky feet, bland food, and denying basic human needs. Somehow, this is supposed to lead to life. If it doesn't feel like it, well too bad. Time to grin-and-bear-it for Jesus' sake. The end.

I've pictured that image of service myself, but when I look at Scripture, I just don't see that as the picture Jesus paints of service or of selflessness. I think "denying ourselves" is more than just eating broth and crackers, sleeping on hard floors, praying the Lord's prayer nineteen times a day, wearing long black robes, or giving up social media and sweets during Lent season.

This type of servitude might *look* super-selfless, but if it's void of the joy Jesus spoke of, is it really the type of abundant life Jesus was talking about?

The fact is this: joy isn't found in mere sacrifice. God is asking to *be* our desire, our greatest joy. Joy is in the fact that we get *more of Jesus* as we sacrifice.

David puts it this way in Psalm 51:16 (NIV):

Open my lips, Lord,
and my mouth will declare your praise.
You do not delight in sacrifice, or I would bring it;
you do not take pleasure in burnt offerings.
My sacrifice, O God, is a broken spirit;

trading in selfish years

a broken and contrite heart
you, God, will not despise.

God isn't happy when we say, "Oh, I'll give up this for you, God! Look at how selfless I'm being!"

No. Instead, His pleasure comes when we say, "I am broken, I am sinful, and I need You. *You* are my only joy and my righteousness."

Joy is not in somehow finding satisfaction in our denial. It's that as we let go of all that we think we desire, we must take in all that Jesus is and ask Him to fill all our empty spaces. Then, only then, do we get true joy.

When we empty ourselves of the world and our sinful desires, we fill up on Jesus. Life becomes brighter, more enlightening, more satisfying because we are more full of God and less full of sin.

If we believe joy is found in strict denial, we are missing the point, and we will run back for something to fill the emptiness because God doesn't desire strict sacrifice. He desires that we desire Him.

Piousness is not the goal; instead, it's a heart set on Christ.

Allow me to paint a new picture, to help you reframe your thoughts on this idea of service in your "free" years. It goes like this:

Jesus wants what is best for you and me. He wants our best so much that He lived and died for us. Part of our best, Scripture says, is *joy*. Soul-deep, head-spinning, heart-thrilling joy. Scripture also makes it clear that joy is found in Jesus—knowing Him, living in Him, seeking Him, praying to Him, giving ourselves over to Him (i.e. *serving* Him).

After all, Jesus Himself performed the greatest act of service of all time, for "the joy set before Him," (Hebrews 12:2, NIV). Jesus' life wasn't lived out of terror, white-knuckling Himself into obedience, trying to appease His holy Father but out of an overflow of love and a desire to honor His Father. He wasn't devoid of joy; His service *was* a joy because it reconciled God and His people.

Through His life and death (i.e.: His service), we can be reconciled to the Trinity. Service for the sake of unity with God was His great joy, even as a human, and so it must be ours as well.

Only then, for the sake of God, Christ, and the Holy Spirit, will we truly throw off selfishness and put on service and servitude.

We weren't made for a self-flagellating life. We weren't made for suffering just for the sake of suffering. We were made for *God* and self-denial for the sake of Holy Spirit-saturation.

So true service, in its purest form, the type of service the Gospel calls me to, can't be something I drag my feet into. Like Christ, a true servant's heart must be for the joy set before the servant. I must have an eternal perspective, something beyond the here and now, something pulling me forward in love. Service to a holy God must mean more than flogging myself or gritting my teeth and making myself memorize a psalm for the seventeenth time even though it means nothing to me.

True service is submitting to the call of the Spirit of God who lives in me, not a fistfight with my flesh.

True service that the Bible talks about has to somehow, someway, lead to true, undeniable joy.

And so, this is the type of service I have found that leads to joy:

When I volunteer my time at my local church and hold tiny babies and coddle them, using that moment to ponder our Father, who cares so deeply for their tiny toes and souls, who knit them together so cutely and preciously and sweetly and innocently—joy.

When I spend my free morning digging deep into God's Word, crying out for Him to reveal Himself, watching His riches unfold in my mind, rather than digging deep into my social media account—joy.

When I use my spring break to see God move, to serve His kingdom through missions, to serve my family through getting to know them and love them more, to use more time in prayer and the Word, to rest my soul in Him—joy.

trading in selfish years

When I dignify my classmates by simply talking to them in class instead of acting like they don't exist while I scroll through Instagram; when I ponder the God who loves them more than their parents could imagine; when I ponder that they could be the lost sheep, one of the ninety-nine when I choose to pray for them daily and watch God do great work in their life—joy.

When I do the opposite of all these things, I trade in joy for emptiness, for some tease of cheap joy.

All of these things require a sacrifice, but the sacrifice is not the point—it is only a means to an end. The point is to gasp in awe at the God of the universe, to make His name great in my heart and in others' hearts.

Christian college students: what if, instead of just using our independence, flexibility, and free time during these years for our own gain and pleasure-seeking, we used them to know Jesus? What if knowing Jesus actually manifested in serving Him? What if serving Him actually started with desiring Him? What if we volunteered more with our local churches, invited our classmates over for dinners, invested time with people who need to know Jesus, spent our free time praying for friends who need Jesus and studying His Word? What if we saw our summers and long winter breaks as a time to invest in the Kingdom, instead of only vacation?* What if we served our classmates with kindness and invited students to our campus ministries and churches, all because we wanted to invite them into our joy? What if we used our one-hour break between classes to pray for healing and revival instead of watching our tenth episode of the week on Netflix?

What if that was how we spent our freedom and independence—to know Him?

To know God is to love God. If we aren't desiring Him, then it's probably because we've forgotten about Him. We might think we know Him, but we don't. We might think we taste Him, but we don't. We might think we are hearing and seeing, but we aren't. Knowing God and loving Him are one in the same.

---

* We all need vacation and relaxation. There is nothing wrong with those things; God even commands that we rest! However, so often, I have thought of my winter breaks and spring breaks as just times to "chill and catch up on sleep" instead of investing in the Kingdom, through rest in God and meditation on who He is, or using some of that time to reach out to lost people. I think there's a better way, a higher calling to view our breaks than simply for our sleep-gain.

contemplations of a collegiate christian

Wouldn't knowing a holy, kind, good God more deeply change us?

Wouldn't His Spirit move us?

Wouldn't we want to sacrifice, for the sake of knowing Him?

After tasting Him more, would we even desire those selfish years?

Change our desires, Lord. Make us desire to serve and honor you above all else. Give us holy eyes; we cry to see our college years as an investment in the kingdom. Give us holy ears; we plead to hear from You.

Change college students for Your glory, we cry.

Change me, Lord, I cry. I need and want more of this. I pant for the stream of living water. I regret the many days I haven't lived and desired like this. I know He's so willing to meet me in this desire, in this angst for something more than selfishness. These are the desires David was talking about (Psalm 37:4). He quenches those who thirst for Him.

If we do this, if we desire Him, He will show up.

When He shows up, mountains move. The earth quakes. Rocks cry out. Praise and singing explode. Hands are raised. Hearts are lifted. Lives are changed. Sins are confessed. Justification cleanses. Sanctification takes root. Love explodes. Purity follows. Joy erupts.

I think our understanding of Jesus would be deeper if we fueled this type of desire, if we dedicated ourselves to knowing Him. I think Christianity would seem less stiff-necked and boring, and we wouldn't constantly be looking for "thrills" in college. I think Christianity would feel a lot less like servitude or being a slave, and a lot more like joy. Like freedom. Like it was indulgent to serve Jesus.

Selflessness offers us more joy than selfishness ever could, so I'm putting the "selfish years" idea behind me. I want to live with true indulgence, getting more of Jesus and less of myself. He really is all I want, and servitude is where joy is found.

trading in selfish years

Then, as joy flows into my bloodstream and spirit, it might even seem just a little bit selfish because it's just that joyful.

FOUR

medicine for an entitled heart

"You are not your own, for you were bought with a price."
The Apostle Paul, I Corinthians 6:19b-20a, ESV

Let me take a moment to acknowledge this: college is a tricky, tricky place for a believer to avoid selfishness and all of its ugly side effects.

Too many times to count, I have let selfishness take over my thoughts, and with it, covetousness, pride, frustration, and discontent followed, even though I didn't realize I was inviting these other companions along for the ride.

There have been far too many times I have lived with the subtle undertone that "I deserve this." Whether it was a scholarship or a job, a particular grade or a particular seat in class, a date with a boy or my professor's approval, a babysitting gig, or a traveling experience, I thought somehow it was unfair if the outcome wasn't in my favor.

However, this sense of entitlement isn't a fruit of the spirit, and it's actually the opposite of Christ-likeness. There was no hint of entitlement in Jesus' character: even as God Himself, He washed the feet of sinners (John 13:1-17). Christ gave up His right to Heaven for the sake of our salvation (Philippians 2:5-8).

My state of entitlement muted my ears to God's voice. I was not asking God where He was leading me. Instead, I assumed my desires were also His: I get what I want. I prayed with an agenda, not with a willing spirit. I was chasing after things that God was not calling me to with little regard for His input. Then, I was frustrated at why nothing was working out, why I felt out-of-place, weary, anxious, low on joy, and massively confused at every turn.

Instead of crawling to His throne and bowing to His guidance, I praised Him during my devotionals and campus ministry worship while so often resenting my circumstances on regular weekday mornings.

In His grace, He opened my eyes to my harmful, entitled heart. He revealed to me that I actually thought I deserved something when I came before His throne in prayer. I had forgotten my great debt He had forgiven, my sins He'd eliminated, my wrongs He'd righted. In my heart of hearts, I thought He actually owed me some sort of grace when I came before His throne.

He eventually revealed my heart to my conscience, through a process called conviction. At a Christian conference I attended one summer, a campus minister pointed out that one of Israel's biggest, most invasive, and gross sins was not only that of distrust and idolatry but that of ingratitude and discontentment, conditions I was all too acquainted with.

Paul takes it as far as to say that being ungrateful is on the same playing field as being brutal, heartless, and "swollen with conceit" (2 Timothy 3:4).

When I realized all of the gifts He had lavished on me had not penetrated my heart, had not caused me to enter the heartfelt posture of bending my knees in honor, I realized that He really does love sinners too well, and I wept over my sin.

I spent weeks reading books, Psalms, and verses on gratitude, on covetousness, on repentance. I spent hours singing worship songs, praising Him for opening my eyes to my sin, thus opening my heart to praise and gratitude.

It was medicine to my soul, sweet and invasive, cleansing, washing me all over: *This is undeserved. This is mercy. This is grace.*

I have found it's much more fun to be grateful and to posture our hearts to come before Him with praise instead of frustration. Sure, He can handle our doubts and questions and cares, and He does so with patient kindness. But gratitude is detoxifying for sick and forgetful humans, like me, who forget how to bend my knees in thankful praise. It's the position humans were designed for; it's why we have knees to bow, hands to raise, eyes to cry, and vocal cords to sing aloud.

medicine for an entitled heart

I found that choosing to praise, even when I am rock-bottom selfish and hard-core coveting, is treatment and medicine for an infected soul. It is an invasion of the reality of my emptiness and His abundance, and He begins filling my emptiness with His Spirit.

This is the beauty of grace: being washed of your sins anew and experiencing a newness of intimacy with the goodness of God.

God's grace heals and cleanses, especially in a culture and season of life where we are constantly taught we deserve everything, right now, with sprinkles on top. It washes us of our greed, rinses our covetousness, refuses the illusion of hard-earned work, releases us of our sense that "I deserve this," and allows our falsely entitled souls to be washed over with a joy unlike we ever could imagine.

This is also what often makes self-entitlement easy and gratitude hard. In a give-and-take society on college campuses, where it seems we are always earning our right to make a living, earning our right to be known, we tend to over-estimate our merit and forget our debt.

We forget that contrite hearts, humble spirits, and servanthood are the places where God meets us; not necessarily in our awards and honors, acceptance speeches, and published research. Through humility, we get life; not in fighting to earn our place, not in calling the shots, not in pulling up our bootstraps and "making something out of ourselves," not in our Western idea of what success means.

This is not where God's grace meets us; it's in our mess and our weakness (2 Corinthians 12:9). God meets with us in our humility, in the brokenness of our own sin, in the down-in-the-mud feelings of "I am gross, and I need a Savior." That's where He met David when he committed adultery, the apostle Paul when he was headed to kill Christians. It's even where He met the thief on the cross. He met them with grace, in their lowest points of sin, when they messed it up big time, and it's where He meets us still.

But we can't get this type of sweet gratitude if we aren't willing to humbly recognize our need and receive grace.

That's what makes grace so hard—it is truly, cringingly humiliating. It's humiliating to admit the reality that, after all our exhausting striving to deserve anything from God, we come up in the red, empty-handed, still deserving wrath and damnation, before a holy God.

It is hard because, ultimately, we did not earn what is ours. It attests that, yes, we drink from an undeserved fountain of living water, and its source has nothing to do with us and has existed long before us. It is scandalously beautiful because we do not deserve to behold His goodness, to snuggle it and soak it in until we are bursting at the seams with forgiveness and love.

Grace is hard because we have to let go of every illusion of "I deserve this," and "my idea would be better," in exchange for humility and the truth of the matter.

Grace wrecks our illusion of entitlement.

Hear me out: you and I do not deserve anything before a Holy God. Our secret pride, our ignorance of His goodness, the hateful thoughts we've harbored against our neighbors, our perversion of His gift of sex, the gossip we feed on—it all disqualifies us because He is so much more beautiful than those things. He is too kind and wonderful to be in the presence of these wrong and twisted acts. They don't just make Him mad; they grieve His heart (Genesis 6:6, Psalm 78:40).

And yet, somehow, if we choose to accept that we are sinners in need of grace, our shame is not the end of the story. The liberating part is the goodness of His character has never depended on our merit. His blessings of mercy and grace have never been and will never be based on our merit. He can be merciful because that's who He is. He took on His own wrath against sin so we didn't have to. It is so paralyzingly wonderful to know we have a God who lavishes the boundless treasure of grace on grimy needy sinners, making them saints. He gives us Himself—still, not because of us—but because of who He is.

I'm learning to embrace grace, push off the deception of entitlement, and clothe myself in grateful praise. This is living in light of the Gospel: calling out our sin for all the nastiness that it is and embracing God for all the mercy He extends. This fuels us to live in step with the Spirit, to love the abundant life He speaks of (John 10:10).

In my life, this looks like confessing my sins, repenting, and being dosed in mercy every day. It's discussing His new, daily mercies with those around me, over packed lunches and cafeteria trays. My friends and I had a tradition of an end-of-the-semester toast where we recalled all the good things over the past few months; it often ended in tears of gratitude and a sweet sense of His kindness and our unworthiness. Kyle and I write all the answered prayers and desires on the side of our refrigerator. It reminds us of God's lavishing of grace on us at every turn in this life. All these things remind me how I don't deserve a life as sweet as this, I don't deserve my friends, I don't deserve my husband, and most immensely of all—I don't deserve the treasure of my God.

I love the process of attributing it all to grace, grace, always grace. Always Jesus—grace embodied.

Ever since God convicted me of ingratitude and entitlement, I often have to pray for Him to reposition my heart. I repeat those simple words to myself, letting a dose of the Gospel flow into my bloodstream, and once again be the medicine for my entitled heart:

Grace, grace, always grace.

Good thing God doesn't treat me according to my merit. Good thing my way isn't God's way of doing things. Good thing He isn't tallying up the costs. Instead, the calculus of grace rules His kingdom:

We deserved destruction, yet He repays us in life. We deserved isolation, yet He calls us family. We deserved hunger, yet He lavishes us with living bread. We deserved nothing, yet He offers us every spiritual gift.

I want to live in this reality more. I'm making this a pillar, a firm foundation for college and beyond. I'm striving for daily gratitude and praise.

A heart stripped of prideful entitlement and filled will gratitude is humbling and beautiful because it is a witness to the reality that this is all by

grace,

grace,

always *grace.*

grace, truth, and freshman year

"God is never said to be patient about things or circumstances. Why? It is because He knows all things. He knows the beginning and the end. He does not have any need of that kind of patience. When we speak of the patience of God, we are not talking about enduring hard times; we are talking about being longsuffering with people."

David Hocking

I am sorely embarrassed by my freshman year self. So much so that I was going to write a chapter noting all of the things I felt I did wrong freshman year to prevent those of you who haven't walked through it from making the same mistakes I did.

I still want you to learn from my mistakes, but I stopped myself from writing the chapter because I could feel the frustration with my past self deep in my soul, and I felt that the chapter would be written out of frustration instead of conviction. So I decided to write this to you, sweet reader, instead. To encourage both you and myself:

As much as I'd love to take back the immature decisions, the dumb flirting, the insecurity that I let rule my actions, and all the times I put prayer and time with God on the backburner, I have to remember and choose to be more amazed by how well God still loved me during that time.

Those decisions weren't acceptable or righteous, and I refuse to make excuses or downplay their repercussions. They hurt God, me, and others around me, no doubt. But when I focus on all the things I've done wrong instead of all the grace of God, I don't improve at all. Focusing on my mistakes doesn't heal me; it actually just makes me more self-focused and self-deprecating.

Replaying past offenses of freshman year and regretting them over again does me no good. What does me good, though, is to ponder God's kindness towards me. In John's account of the Gospel, He says this:

> *The Word became flesh and made his dwelling among us.*
> *We have seen his glory, the glory of the one and only Son,*
> *who came from the Father, full of grace and truth.*
> John 1:14, NIV

God's glory, revealed to us in His son, is full of grace and truth. This is one of the most central things about God: He is grace and truth perfected.

When we consider our mistakes, we need to examine and acknowledge the mistake, in order that appropriate grace can be applied to it. This is the glory of God, that He is the perfect healer. In His truth, He doesn't turn a blind eye to our sin and immaturities; He calls them out for what they are. In His grace, He doesn't leave us damned in our shortcomings.

So when I think about freshman year, I realize I need to embody both grace and truth: I was immature and sinful in a million ways, but He was with me, calling me back to Himself, loving me all the while. His love overrules my failings because, for the believer, grace always abounds beyond our sin (Romans 5:20).

I don't think I'll ever completely escape regret here on this earth. Now, I also look back on my sophomore year and junior year and think, "I was so immature about that." And I will look back, in a few years, and think the same thing about my season now, right after graduation.

But God is both truthful and gracious for our growth. God is also the essence of love, and the very first thing Paul has to say about love is that it is patient (1 Corinthians 13:4). What a statement to begin with. God doesn't shove us into growth; He, like a wise mentor and counselor, gently and quietly leads us there.

So what would I say to freshman year self in light of that?

"Don't make excuses for your present immaturity, MM. Seek God's face more, ponder God more than you ponder theology itself, stop looking at the news and being mad at politics, stop caring what boys think so much, stop trying to gain validation by proving your intelligence to everyone because you don't have anything to prove. Your God has given you all the approval, love, and acceptance you need. Just get to know Him more, and the rest of this won't be so daunting, won't hold so much weight in your soul."

But what I am saying to myself now is this:
Let go of what is behind because He saw those sins, called you out of them, and gave you grace to move past them. Love keeps no record of wrong, so stop with all the replaying. Dig deep into His present grace, all the maturity He is growing in you in this season. Bask in the love He is offering you in the here and now.

My hope is, just maybe, if I do that, I won't have quite so much to regret in a few years.

SIX

here is your invitation

Therefore, since we are surrounded by such a great cloud of witness-es, let us throw off everything that hinders and the sin that so easily entangles. And let us run with perseverance the race marked out for us, fixing our eyes on Jesus, the pioneer and perfecter of faith.

Hebrews 12:1, NIV

I became a believer and grew in the faith in a Christian subculture that was very good at not being legalistic. Actually, we were so good at not being legalistic, we became legalistic about not being legalistic.*

Meaning that, if anyone ever thought they might need to give up something in order to deepen their relationship with Christ, albeit that it wasn't inherently sinful, then we were the first to say, "But ____ is also a gift from God! Don't feel guilty about it! Enjoy His good gifts!"

And yes, this is true. God has given us good gifts, and we should enjoy them to His glory—meaning, enjoy them, in order to enjoy Him more. However, these good gifts can often get in the way of our intimacy with Him. We linger with the gifts longer than we linger in His presence. We trust the gifts just a little more than we trust Him.

This gift might not even be a full-blown idol *yet*, but it's inching its way into

---

For those of you who are confused by this: while most kids were busy not cussing, smok-ing, or drinking, it was often assumed in my subculture that God's grace covered me even more because of these things. This is a theological fallacy called "cheap grace" and is addressed in Dietrich Bonhoeffer's "The Cost of Discipleship" and by the Apostle Paul in Romans 6.

the category. It becomes a bit more of a habit with each passing day, grabs a little bit tighter onto your affections, becomes a little more difficult to loosen your grip on, takes a little bit more of your day, until suddenly you are turning to *it* for fulfillment and not Christ. The God who formed you becomes second. The gift comes first. An idol has been successfully manufactured in the factory of your heart.

I have often allowed unhelpful barriers to stand between me and God in the name of "not being legalistic."*

In college (and in the world in general), the distractions and temptations for idols are forever-present, always tempting, and nagging. They don't let up. You can't just trust your time, money, and efforts to naturally be for Christ each day. You have to work towards it and strategize about how to set your mind on things above. This is true of any season, but college is a breeding ground for selfishness and idols, as I've discussed in chapters before.

So, I wanted to write you the invitation I needed in college. Allow me to take a moment to invite you to break down all the barriers that stand between you and Christ on any given day.

Is a barrier the Netflix show that you've seen five times already? How about the social media app you can't seem to stop clicking on? The significant other that never cared much for God? Your sorority or fraternity?

Well, here is your chance, the answer to prayer you've been waiting for: let it go. Give it up. Put it down. Break down the barrier. The pain of sacrifice is worth the intimacy with God. *He* is worth it.

Take it from Jesus Himself, in more startling terms, in Mark 9:47 (ESV):

"And if your eye causes you to sin, tear it out. It is better for you to enter the kingdom of heaven with one eye than with two eyes to be thrown into hell."

Better for us to let go of Netflix, the boyfriend/girlfriend, the social club than to give up another moment of intimacy with God.

---

* *Paul actually addresses this idea head-on in 1 Corinthians 10. Go there for a whole passage on the ways we should use our freedom.*

here is your invitation

Now, if you're like me, the temptation is to be afraid of letting go—not because I am afraid of getting intimate with God. I want that deeply. It's because I'm afraid of failing, and I'm afraid God won't follow through on His intimacy.

a)   afraid of failing

b)   afraid the intimacy won't even happen

Let's address the fear of failure first by saying this encouraging statement: you will likely fail. (I know, I know. "Don't be too encouraging, Mary Mad!")

Failure is a reality. Because we are human, and idols and distractions aren't easily cast down, we will stumble along the way. If you are in Christ, God will ultimately win this battle, but our enemy isn't going to make it easy. You will cringe when you delete the app, when you resign from the social club, when you break up with the girlfriend/boyfriend. You might think, "How will I be able to do this?" You will probably even go back to them, once, twice, or seven times, looking for some relief.

Don't seek failure but definitely don't fear it. Don't refuse to fight simply because you're afraid you might get knocked down a couple of times. Get back up. Punch the Enemy in the face again. Tell him victory is in Christ. Christ will win His people over. He can't keep you from Christ.

Now, to address the second point: being afraid God won't show up.

After you've taken the first step to getting rid of the distractions or idols, you try to fill that void with prayer, the Word, fellowship with other Christians, etc., and you don't *feel* it just yet. You don't feel *Him* just yet. You just left behind all those idols, and intimacy with God seems elusive.

This is not the time to give up. God has a promise for you in Hebrews 11:6 (NIV), Christian:

> *And without faith it is impossible to please God, because*
> *anyone who comes to Him must believe that He exists*
> *and that He rewards those who earnestly seek Him.*

Do you hear that? Perseverance. He rewards those who *earnestly* seek Him.

contemplations of a collegiate christian

Not those who casually, half-heartedly, every-now-and-again seek Him. He rewards the person who knocks—even bangs—on His door, over and over and over again; the one who shows up and gets ready to fight like Jacob and says, "I'm not leaving until You bless me with Yourself, God." You can take His word for it. Get your whole heart involved in the fight, and the Word promises us He *will* show up.*

Maybe it won't be the first time, the first month, the first prayer. Maybe it won't be the fiftieth, but He will come if you keep showing up in faith, knocking at His door, reminding Him of His promise. And when He does show, you will be so grateful you left behind your idol for the presence of the living God. He will make those idols look like dirt and grime compared to knowing Him.

So there's your invitation, college student, to "throw off the sin that clings so closely"—every distraction and idol—in order to run this sanctification race with perseverance, as the author of Hebrews encourages us.

Perseverance assumes the race won't be easy. It will hurt at times, but you aren't in this alone. You fall down, He helps you back up. You skin your knees, He heals. You don't know which way to turn, He guides you.

In the midst of it all, "fixing our eyes on Jesus, the pioneer and perfecter of faith" is where victory lies. If we do this, our victory is certain.

Eyes on the prize, collegiate Christian.

Eyes on Him.

---

* *For more on this idea of continuous asking of God, study the story of the persistent widow in Luke 18:1-8.*

SEVEN

the lighthouse

*For God, who said, "Let there be light in the darkness," has made
this light shine in our hearts so we could know the glory of
God that is seen in the face of Jesus Christ. We now have this
light shining in our hearts, but we ourselves are like fragile
clay jars containing this great treasure. This makes it clear
that our great power is from God, not from ourselves.*

The Apostle Paul, II Corinthians 4: 6-7, NIV

College students live in all sorts of areas: dorm rooms, condos, apartments,
mobile homes, rental houses, with the families they nanny for, at their parents'
places, even in small guest homes attached to their churches. There's no short-
age of options, and I have experienced about half of these places. However, my
favorite and most memorable experience, one that I will praise God for the rest
of my life, is living in a home with five of my closest friends.

I hope you will allow me to indulge myself for a chapter, as I want to tell you a
little bit about our home, just because it was super special to me, and I love to
share the story. I don't want you to desire *my* story though; I want you to desire
God's story for *your* life. I want the both of us to live with open hands for His
plan for housing, even if it looks nothing like that of others. But as for one of
my sweetest college experiences, here it is:

Housing is a big deal in college. It sets the tone for the academic year. The
people you live with can either make your residence feel like a prison cell, only
a house, or if you get really lucky, a home. In my circumstances, after living in
a dorm room for two years, my idea of a roommate was: I get my room, they
get theirs. We run into each other in the kitchenette and split chores. We talk

sometimes. Maybe we laugh. Hopefully, we are friends.

However, junior year changed my perspective for the better. I'd never imagined a housing situation could be so sanctifying and satisfying until then. Besides meeting and marrying my husband, living on 707 Whitfield with those five girls, was the most treasured experience of my collegiate time.

Here is our story:

After finding a house with five bedrooms, my best friend and I recruited four other girls to live with us. A couple of us were good friends, some of us kind of knew each other, and others of us had only spoken a few words here and there.

Including me, the full count in our home was six girls. Yes, you read that correctly—six roommates, one home. For some, that might seem like five more roommates than they would prefer, and some days, I thought so too. We often laughed at people's flabbergasted faces when we told them how many roommates we had. Yet, instead of a housing situation that might have seemed destined for disaster, the Lord made it one of the greatest blessings in our college lives.

Our two-story home was white both inside and out, with sixteen windows, including two window seats, a wall of windows in our living room, and windows for doors. Plus, we strung Christmas lights that twinkled and sparkled on the porch at night. Considering all the brightness, we decided to christen our home "The Lighthouse." It turned out to be the perfect name as, literally, our home filled with sunlight daily, and, metaphorically, God used the Lighthouse to illuminate the dark areas we carried with us through the doors.

In many college living situations, rooms are fought after and won with money. For us, the room assignments were surprisingly the easiest part: each room fit each of our personalities like a favorite t-shirt.

I want to take a moment to introduce five ladies that changed me forever:

Alli lived in the front room, right next to the front door. It was the most fitting because she was the most welcoming roommate. Just bring a stranger into our doors, and by the end of the conversation, she would be able to name their grandparents on both sides and tell you their sorrows like their story had become her own. Many afternoons and mornings, you could walk by her open door and find her digging into Scripture, writing down verses on note cards, taping them on her wall, and tattooing them on her heart. She would look intent, legs crossed, hand cupping her chin, eyes four inches from the page. If her shirt was too big, it just might expose the crescent moon tattoo on her shoulder that she got on a whim when she was 18. If you knocked and peeked inside, she would look up briefly from the Scripture to smile at you and ask about your day because she truly cared. Still, in that moment, she would be trying to balance God's whispering and the debriefing of your day. So unless it was a terribly awful day, you would choose to smile and let her be, praying that one day you would crave His Word and trust Him as Allison Marie Michaels does.

Kendra claimed the room right off the living room. It had three giant windows on a curved wall that fit her tan loveseat like a glove. She purchased that loveseat for $30 at a garage sale. She was really proud of that purchase, and we were really proud too. So proud, in fact, that every guest who toured our home would be required to sit on it. It's still the softest, most smooshy couch one will ever encounter—I'm sure of it. If you are short enough or willing enough to curl up, it's the shotgun seat during a sleepover, and everyone wants dibs—including Kendra.

The best part of it, though, was that if you were up late at night, Kendra Leigh Sanders would most definitely be up too. And if the world was dark and you were weary, you could tip-toe to Kendra's room, and the light would always be on. Knock, enter, and throw your weak bones on that couch, and no matter how tired her eyes were, and no matter how frustrated she was with her homework, she would weave her hands together, briefly close her eyes, shrug her slender shoulders, take a releasing exhale, turn her face towards you, and with a soft-smile, sweetly tease you about something, and ask about your day. There, on that loveseat, you would begin to rest your eyes and your heart.

Many counseling sessions and theological discussions were had on that couch, and no matter what you were going through, she wasn't going to hold back on the truth or the love of her God. The half-awake conversation would be warmly snuggled in her kindness until you both decided that morning was too close, and you begrudgingly snuck off to your bed, which undoubtedly paled in comparison to the loveseat. After leaving Kendra's room, I'd always fall asleep hard and fast, mind at ease, with a new perspective and a new hope. It's not called a "loveseat" for any old reason, and it's no coincidence that our loveseat lived in

contemplations of a collegiate christian

Kendra Sanders' room.

Amber resided in the back room, which we all decided made sense because she is the most introverted of all of us. In fact, her favorite word is "sequester." An art major, walking into her room was like walking into a gallery or an indie record store. Sketches of moons and geometric drawings lined the wall above her mahogany dresser. A map of Malawi, Africa, the place where she spent seven years of her childhood as a missionary kid, sat above her bookshelf, which was governed by Ernest Hemingway. The record player crowned the top of a collection of vinyl from old rock bands, Tame Impala, and our favorite garage-boy band, Mom Jeans. Her artsy-ness peeked through every corner of that room, which makes sense because Amber speaks her love through art. She is a unique communicator, and unlike the rest of us, would rarely squeal over anything or tell a monologue about her day. Instead, you could find her excitement and care packaged in paper and ink: gifting you your favorite piece of her artwork from the semester, lending out her favorite classic novel with a smile, playing you her favorite album her father played when she was a little girl, or cutting out her favorite comics from the New Yorker and taping them to your bathroom mirror.

As for affection, she might sweetly punch you with a giggle after you did something silly or come ruffle your hair, putting her chin on your head if she was especially feeling the love. If you knocked on her door, she would probably not be there because she was in the studio, making beautiful things out of otherwise meaningless items. However, if you were so lucky as to hear a muffled, "Yeah?" Then, there were few greater blessings than to sit on Amber Elizabeth McDonald's bed and stay for a while. We jokingly called Amber our dad because, like a father, we often left Amber's room with a giggle and an affirming sense that we belonged to her.

The left upper room belonged to Kelley. Kelley was the eldest of all of us, and in her extra two years of life, she became well-versed in literature, movies, beer, food, and all things British, yet, she never once made us feel less than if our knowledge and experience didn't match hers. In fact, she was one of those people that, as Lord Crawley in Downton Abbey said, will "love you forever if you let her." I never heard Kelley report an ill action of someone without promptly assuming their best intentions. In her room, you would find a million coffee cups from weeks past, which she would inevitably be ashamed of. Because as we all have our quirks, Kelley's thing was leaving coffee cups upstairs for a long, long time, until mold began to form. But, we would all rush to hush her words when she went into her shame-talk about the cups because we found that the reason she left coffee cups upstairs was because she was too busy moving on to other things: loving the next person, baking the next loaf of bread, praying the next prayer, inviting in the next stranger, or tending to the next person who had had a sad day. And there was nothing we wanted more in our lives than the Kelley Victoria Murphree who left behind coffee cups for people.

The fifth and last room was occupied by Sara Beth and me. Our room was like a shoebox: just wide, long, and tall enough to fit its contents. It's like God decided on that room with us in mind. We are the exact same height—five feet, two and a half inches—and her six-foot, seven-inch boyfriend did not find our twin beds or the ceiling height to be nearly as comfortable as we did. S.B. and I sometimes joked we were practically the same person, and in many ways, this was true. We shared favorite authors, many favorite songs, an intense passion for adventure, many similar thoughts on life, and the same confused excitement about where our passions were leading us. There have been numerous times when she'd shared her thoughts with me, and I felt like she'd been stealing my diary at night.

However, our differences were stark in brilliant and complementing ways. My favorite distinction was that while I was one for confrontation, S.B. was a peacemaker at heart. She had the ability to lay down all arms and give up her own pride in order to make the best of a situation. You asked her for an inch, and she would freely offer up a mile, embodying Luke 6:29 like no one else I had ever seen. S.B. was the type of person who would not only pick you up from campus just because she was out and about, but she would also offer to take you to get ice cream and hold your soul for a moment if the day had been too heavy. She would always let you have your space, but if you offered up your worries and joys, she would hold them with the utmost regard. In college, Sara Beth Pritchard was willing to sacrifice everything—sleep, class, money, work—for the things that mattered most like spontaneous prayer and working through problems with the people she loved.

S.B.'s side of the room was full of wildflowers from the side of the road, essential oils, and plenty of polaroids. She was an amazing photographer and saw the world in ways that most people cannot imagine until they view her work. She was quick to assume the best in those around her, no matter their history, and this manifested in her work. She saw you and me and others the way we only wished we saw ourselves, the way I think God probably sees us, and she captured this perfectly in film. On days when I was my own worst critic, Sara Beth Pritchard made me look at myself through Jesus' eyes, simultaneously mourning my brokenness and speaking truth and life into my dry and heavy bones.

My side of the room was less decorated in comparison to S.B.'s, mostly because my books were scattered all throughout the house, a habit kindly tolerated by my roommates. The Lord has given me a soul that is constantly captured by basically every discipline of study. No subject is mundane or boring in my mind—from astronomy to geography to theology to quantum physics and especially cognitive psychology. I have a passion for learning about stuff, any type of stuff—people, places, ideas, inventions, scientific discoveries, etc.— then rambling about it to whoever will listen. My roommates were gracious to be the listeners so often, hearing my long-winded rambles about all the things I'd learned that day at school. For that simple kindness, I am eternally grateful.

These were the ladies of 707 Whitfield Street, who God gave me for one short year, and who—in that one short year—changed my life forever.

Now, after reading this, I hope you walk away hopeful for the next season of housing or living in a new place, or something of the like. I hope you dream it up with God, pray for deep relationships, give Him those hopes and dreams, and patiently watch as He either paints them into life or transforms them into something more complex and beautiful than you could have brainstormed.

But, if after reading this, and you are tempted to think for a moment that we are perfect, your housing situation could never look like ours, or you're hopeless and despairing because you think you missed out on something, please don't. If you can't get that out of your head, close this book, walk away, and pray for contentment and hope. God's best place for you is the one you are placed in, not the one He's placed someone else in.

Know that I painted these pictures of these women for you because it's the story of a changed perspective, of what happens when God changes your mind. I thought I wanted a room to myself and a house with maybe two roommates— but I was wrong. I thought I was getting decent roommates, not sisters in Christ. And then God changed me, and now I see them as I wrote above: beautiful, strong, kind, talented, complex, rich, radiant daughters of God, my sisters. The flip side of our strengths are hurtful flaws. It took us many months of very involved friendship, lots of hurts and apologies, lots of hard and deep conversation, and plenty of regular bonding time to get to the point where we could laugh, talk, and tease the way we do to this day. We are always going to have our days of frustration with each other. We are human and fallen, and we hurt each other, say our apologies, and try to move on. Sometimes we fail at it, falling into bitterness, but we always try again and again. Learning to say "I'm sorry," mend our wrongs, and look closely to examine what God is doing in our relationships is a skill we must all hone. God put this perspective and fierce love in our hearts for one another, but it wasn't without work.

Because of our shared space and shared lives, because of those moments of tension followed by "I'm sorry" and "Can we try this again," I know more of how to love when it's hard to like, how to forgive when you can't forget, how to grant someone the benefit of the doubt, how to give until it hurts, how to be family to strangers.

Through this Lighthouse, Christ has taught me what light really does:

Light exposes,

Light invades,

Light cleanses,

Light requires a response,

Light shines in the darkness,

Light builds friendships,

Light builds houses,

Light builds homes.

I pray He does something wonderful and surprising in your roommates and friendships, and I hope you are open to whatever it is, no matter how ordinary or how extraordinary your arrangement looks. I never planned on living in the Lighthouse, but through this divine construction of our home, He taught us how to expose, invade, cleanse, respond, shine love and truth out into a dark, aching world and into our own hearts when we needed it the very most.

Through light, God built friendships that moved us into a house and made it a home.

EIGHT

the missing piece
of friendship

*"When the only person that truly knows all about us is the person
who uses our hairbrush, we are easy pickings for the Enemy,
ripe for being outmaneuvered and outsmarted. That's how we
remain slaves to our repeated failures, by basically resisting the
redeeming love of God and the needed, encouraging support of
others. Because even if we're as much as 99 percent known (or
much less, as is more often the case) to our spouse, our friends,
our family, and the people around us, we are still not fully known."*

Matt Chandler, *Recovering Redemption*

Most friendships in college seem to go like this: you meet, you have a few
things in common, maybe even a lot, so you talk about them. You might know
the same people, you might even do the same hobbies or have similar majors.

You then exchange numbers and invite each other to coffee, sit by each other
in class, go check out a Bible study together, and attend the same late-night
hangouts. Eventually, you build a collection of memories and laughs, like when
you both ate cereal and Skittles for dinner, or when you invited a random guy
to your friend's cabin, and he ended up chugging a beer and jumping into a
freezing lake in his underwear all by himself because he wanted to look cool,
but it was actually just really awkward. Or the time you wore ribbons braided
into your hair because you thought it'd be cute. (Wrong.) Or the time you accidentally told your crush that you'd tried ketchup for lotion like Miley Stewart
did on *Hannah Montana*. (Too soon.) You build these memories together, and
they weave together through time to create a safety net for your emotions and
personality. You begin to share some of your unpopular, tiny secrets with one

another, your small fears, cares, concerns, and prayers—the ones you might not post on the internet but nothing too jolting or upsetting.

Oftentimes, it stops there though. At the collection of memories, a lot of laughter, and some small fears shared, there comes a halt in the progression. Tiny exposings and small worries confessed, it seems like there's enough to have an authentic relationship, so you halt the momentum for fear of being known any more than this. You are close now. You tell each other difficult things, but not too difficult; this seems like it will do for a fulfilling friendship. You are content enough with being this amount of known but no more. So, you keep the things to yourself that make you cry into your pillow at night or the sin you think about every morning when you wake up. Those things are only for you to know. Your friends wouldn't understand, and they would think you're disgusting or a little too much to handle if you told them. It's better not to. You don't want to mess up the relationship or their perception of you, so you figure it's better to keep it only this deep.

This is not a shallow friendship. You aren't a surface-level friend, but it is what I would like to call a just-below-the-surface-level friendship. Just honest enough to seem like you're being really authentic, but not the painful, hard, this-makes-me-feel-so-hopeless -and-worthless-I-want-to-cry-on-your-lap type of honesty. Not the please-preach-the -gospel-to-me-now type.

This is a stagnant friendship. It's a waist-deep friendship that doesn't want to move forward.

I know all about this because I've been there. I've been the person who was never truly honest with my closest friends about my guilt, doubts, fears, and hurts when the time came to dig deeper and know each other more. I was just partially honest, just enough to squeak by, all the while tricking myself into thinking I was really being authentic.

But then one day, by God's providence, and through a sermon via podcast, I felt the push to take the things that weighed heavily on my heart and share them with my friend. I took the leap, and through gritted teeth and many tears, I exposed the truest version of myself: the shame I felt about my hidden body image and food issues, the anxieties I didn't want to admit I had, my most looming fears and nightmares about my worth. I shared my heartaches and largest embarrassments that I didn't know what to do with. I didn't know what would happen after that; I just knew I needed to walk through that moment of vulnerability.

Because my friend loved me like Jesus, I was met with hugs, prayers, and the Gospel story recounted anew. Little did I know my snotty, red-faced confession, was where my deepest friendship began. It's where the good, sweet, eternal stuff began to sprout in our friendship, and it began to leak into every other part of my life. It's where Jesus met me.

Up until this point, we were friends. It was a fun and nice bond, but there came a point where I had to step a little deeper into the ocean of risk. There came a time when I spoke out loud, into the air, the "one percent" I wanted to hide from, the percent that I believed would create a wall between me and her—and ultimately, that I believed created a wall between me and Jesus.

Until I opened up to my friends about my one percent, our friendships were only good. They weren't soul-deep, sanctifying and satisfying, and that's what I was craving in my bones.

We all have one, two, maybe a few things we want to hide, our "one percent" we want to cover up, no matter the cost. Whatever this is for you, if you never speak these out loud, you will settle for good friendships, instead of wonderful and awe-inspiring friendships. Until you say that thing, until you tell them about the person you loved who left and the abandonment eating away at your core, until you tell them about how you can't get over your toxic relationship with food, waking up every day remembering you have to face the mirror, until you tell them about your misuse of sex or abuse that someone committed against you, these things will hold you and your friendship captive, stagnant, only ankle-deep. You will skim the surface of friendship, cheating yourself and your friend of the full gift.

If you are the person who holds back the one percent to the dearest friend who deeply loves you and loves Jesus so much, I beg you, please say it. Spit it out, even it comes out in fumbles and ummms and sobs. Even if you're so embarrassed about how embarrassed you are. That's okay. You don't have to know what comes next; you just need to step into the moment of exposure. The other side will take care of itself. Ask Him to teach you how to confess fully and truthfully, without a sugar-coated version and "I'm fine." If you fully submit to the moment and your friend meets you with truth and love, on the other side of that moment, is healing. More importantly, He promises us in James 5:16 (ESV, emphasis added):

> *Therefore, confess your sins to one another and pray*
> *for one another, that you may be healed.*

If you are the person who is receiving that one percent, listen and empathize. The Lord honors this. Maybe you're afraid of messing things up and saying the wrong thing. His greatness is made perfect when we feel inadequate (2 Corinthians 12:9). Ask Him to teach you to love and show grace to your shame-struck friend. Look at how Jesus dealt with shame. Model Him. It will be a great honor, a life-giving moment if we don't shy away, trusting that He is bigger than our sin, shame, and fears.

Friendship is risky, and sometimes your friend might not know how to best love you at this moment. But you also might not know how to love them well just yet, and that's okay. This is a learning process. You might not get it right the first time but be patient and kind with one another. Pray together. Learn each other's triggers and pay careful attention to be gentle with them. God is calling us deeper into a relationship with Him—we know this. But He is also calling us into relationship with one another, and it's such a gift if we choose to live out this lesson.

The nature of college life and schedule often makes it such a pivotal and convenient time for friendship. Please don't waste this time on surface-level conversations and relationships. Fun and games are great, but call yourself and your friends to something higher, more wonderful, more meaningful, something deep and moving and lasting. Friendship can serve not only as a gift but also as gird—a sword against the enemy's attacks of secret shame and sin. This type of relationship is the Gospel in action, something worthy of our time, something which will outlast these four years.

It matters, this type of friendship. Not only are we rehearsing for future adulthood, but this type of relationship matters in the here and now. Value it. Invest in it. You are going to need authentic friends who tell you the hard stuff. You are going to need to be vulnerable with the people who love you and have the people you love be vulnerable right back, calling you out of darkness and into the light.

the missing piece of friendship

True friendship, the type where you are 100%, fully, truly known, in all your sainthood and in your sin, will radically change your sanctification journey. The Enemy's attacks of shame and secret sin are exposed when we confess them, bringing them into the light to examine and fight them with friends. This will change the game in your fight against the flesh, fight against yourself, fight against the enemy.

I believe this type of vulnerable friendship is the missing piece to good, life-giving, joy-abundant friendships—ones that call us from darkness into light. It's nothing new, either. It's literally as old as time, starting in the Garden of Eden, when God called Adam and Eve to admit their fault and to stop hiding from Him.

And so what's the key to this type of friendship?

Confession.

Confession is firstly admitting the ways we've obviously sinned against God and others, in our thoughts, attitudes, words, and actions. It's where we admit the things we've done and that are in the past, sure. But it's also when we admit the sins that seem too deeply woven, too gripping for us to know where to begin to deal with them. It's speaking out loud the thoughts that haunt us at night, telling the toxic thought patterns we go down on a weekly basis, and putting words to all the ways we hurt for what might seem like no reason at all.

Confession is crushing and reviving all at once. It shines a light into the darkness, making you squint with pain often but allowing you to take a hard look at the truth of your condition for what it is, not what the darkness makes it look like. It lightens up the burden, allowing someone to bear it with you, to help you make sense of it, to help you find the Gospel truth in it, to help you give it back to Jesus and start new.

Without confessing to our Christian confidants, we will hide and be a slave to the enemy's lies. This practice is vital in my relationship with my close friends, my relationship with my Church family, my relationship with my husband, and my relationship with God Himself.

Honest confession in the context of a gracious, loving, and prayerful community leads to healing. It leads to life.

So maybe you're sitting there, right now, reading these words and thinking, "I could never tell them that part of me. I just couldn't."

Let me tell you this: there's a reason few people do it. You will dread the moment of confession. You will want to run away, act like everything is okay, and try to convince yourself that you can pull yourself together alone this time. You will want to hide, especially the first time. You might even wonder, "Why in the heck did I do this?" right after it happens. You might think, "That really hurt and I just feel raw—the end."

But this is part of the process. It's a tool in sanctification, so go to your close, loving, Christ-like friends anyway. Text them right this moment, while you have the courage, and tell them you need to see them. Share this chapter with them. Once you spew it out, even if it's through heaving sobs, if they are good friends, and they know the kindness of their Savior, they will meet you with grace and love and hugs and kisses and kindness. And you might not feel it right in the moment, but eventually, you will feel some release. The situation might feel even heavier as you look it in the face, but you now have someone to bear it with, someone to speak truth and love and forgiveness into it. You have someone to call you out of darkness and into light, out of sin and into holiness. Sin loses its power in the light. And you might still feel like a slave today, but slowly, you will grow out of that identity. God's voice of love will become bigger.

It all starts here, in this pivotal moment of confession.

True confession is the key to the closer-than-a-brother type of friendship. This leads to the good stuff.

So, if you get anything out of this book, please get this: good, Christ-centered, shame-eradicating, confession-and-love relationships will change your college experience (and your life) like nothing else, second to a deep reliance on Jesus.

Don't deprive others or cheat yourself. It will be scary, but I promise you, it is worth it. I am deeply thankful I learned this lesson in college. I'm leaving behind these college years with friends who I know I can call and confess to, no matter how heavy my heart is, and we can fight this, through the Holy Spirit's power and prayer, together.

the missing piece of friendship

College is such a wonderful time to start this, to get really serious about confession in your friendships. You will likely never have so many friends all at once. (Or have so many to choose from!) Take advantage of it, for yourself and for others. Find some safe people to confess to. Use this short amount of time to know others and be known by them, to be pointed to a living God, and to point others. It's the most beautiful thing; I promise. Make the most of this season. Use this time, and don't cheat these friendships. Let them be complete and full.

Make confession a foundation in your friendships.

Call each other out of darkness and into light.

This is what makes the difference in relationships.

This is the higher calling: to live out the Gospel together, growing in holiness.

This, I believe, is the missing piece to friendship.

NINE

bleeding shame

"Like her, with hopes and fears we come,
To touch you if we may
Oh send us not despairing home
Send none unhealed away."
William Cowper, "Heal Us," 1779

If there is one terrible and sad illness that dominates adolescents and adolescent-turning-adults, it is the nauseating, unspeakable sickness of shame. If you didn't catch it in the last chapter, maybe this one will help you process it a little further. It's an important theme, so I am going to give it two chapters. It deserves the attention. If you weren't convinced by the last chapter that you need to practice confession in college, here's my last call in this book.

Really, shame is true for any and all age groups—from tiny five-year-olds to centenarians. However, it seems to be the case that, unless there is a paradigm shift during later life, the thought habits we activate in our late teens and twenties hold the strongest, including those regarding shame.

I don't have any new thoughts to offer on shame in general. I know that Jesus ultimately heals all shame. I do think that confession, as I said before, helps us rid ourselves of bad sin patterns that force us into shame (James 5:16). I think older, wiser people have done a really good job at the conversation in recent years, and I'm proud of our generation for choosing to speak life and light into others' lives instead of choosing silence. I am proud of all the echoes of "me too" and the "I get that" and the "I don't understand fully, but I'm going to try to understand" as we fight the good fight against sin, darkness, and its lies. This focus on eradicating shame will be a marker of our generation, I believe, and I think that's really worth something.

My friends and I have spent a lot of time listening to those really wise people talk about shame—pastors, psychologists, authors and speakers, the people who have walked through deep seasons of shame and much-too-common trauma. We have taken time to read the accounts of Jesus speaking the perfect union of truth and love into others' shame. We are trying hard to do the messy work of figuring out what lies we have believed and untangling the inherent confusion and misinformation they hold. When we think we find a really good podcast on shame, we text each other in the middle, before we have even gotten ten minutes in, just because shame-eradication gets our blood pumping, our spirits excited. And of course, the most difficult task of all, we invite one another to confess all our specific guilts, and we make it a habit to confess ourselves.

I have learned it's vital that I identify the sins and guilt I carry and drag them into the light. Because, if unmonitored, they will cause me to rot, hiding from myself, others, and Jesus without warning and without apologies. With no habit of heart-examination, I will fall deep into shame without even noticing the tumble.

It's hard and deeply tangible work, this sin-and-shame surgery. There's a lot of stamina and materials involved: brutal honesty, salty tears, stumbling words and intense hugs, late-night conversations, and another double dosage of tears and kindness and grace. There have been many times when I would have rather walked away from the conversation, whether with myself or someone else, to take a nap or just ignore the hurt.

But shame is all too relevant to my life, to my friends' lives, to other college-aged people, to adults, to humanity, for me to walk away from the conversation. This de-shaming is too important a work, and Jesus cares far too much about calling people out of shame and dignifying people, for me to act like it doesn't exist.

So, college students, hear me out: get friends who talk about sin and shame. Pray to find them if you haven't yet. Get on your knees and ask for them. Find a way to confess your specific sins, admit your specific shames, and give them the opportunity to do the same. Within a safe space, this will cause your friendships to explode, and this is where you will find the person who "sticks closer than a brother" (Proverbs 18:24).

Because, like a sickness, if specific shames are not often examined, openly diagnosed, and sanitized by the love of Jesus, they will undoubtedly fester. They will infect our souls, making us sick, causing us to hurt and hide from the people who love us best. They will spoil our belief in new life, blind us to all the freeing, tear-heavy, and eye-lifting moments Jesus so openly offers through His shame-execution. Ultimately, they will steal all the joy we are invited to bask in during our college years and beyond. They will rob us of victory in Christ.

I've found shame-webs to be intertwined in my daily life, tightly wound, and having the potential to squeeze out all Gospel truth on the personal level. And if I don't allow Jesus and Christian friends to speak into my shame, I will carry it around with me like a backpack or my student I.D.—into my dorm room, my lecture halls, football games, parties, Bible studies, friendships, romantic relationships, and my todays and tomorrows.

Without asking my permission, shame will follow me, and I will wear it like a cloak—whether I like it or not.

As college students, you are often encouraged to "find yourself" and "create your own life" during this season. I think there's a place for recreation, of course. But few Christians mention how you might have to allow Jesus to radically deconstruct and reconstruct your beliefs about Him, others, and yourself in order to begin anew. No one told me that, even more important than my grades or even a degree, is this de- and re-constructing about who God is and who I am in light of His Truth and how it would really sky-rocket once I hit adulthood. No one mentioned that college is more of a trip in sanctification, in pruning, than in the "time of your life."

As a college student, I had to get my hands messy, trying to de-tangle a complex web of past scars and to get rid of present sin. We all carry some shame, whether it's regarding relational issues, bad sports or extracurricular experiences, past heartbreaks and bullying, or destructive cultural messages. And this isn't just for those who have had particularly difficult lives; I know I haven't. It's simply for humans, those of us living in a fallen world. That's all of us.

But Jesus came to free us from shame, and something has got to change.

contemplations of a collegiate christian

So, we all need to talk about it.

Freedom is part of the Christian life. And the process of walking into full freedom means pulling our sin and shame into the light, calling it out for what it is, walking away from it, and saying "you don't define me anymore; Christ does." This is a huge part of maturing as a Christian, and therefore, it's a vital part of college for Christians, where we are learning what it means to grow into adult Christians.

Contrary to what I once believed, starting at university and finding a new social life did not fix previous shames or naturally make me mature. Maturity, a new season of life, a new growth in my spirit, was a decision I had to step into.

There is a lie that a "fresh new start" awaits all who go off to college. Though a new setting can be helpful, you are still the same person, with the same harms, in the same skin, and bearing the same soul. A new town will not fix your past hurts that you carry. A new situation will not change your heart's situation.

The only "fresh new start" begins when we meet Jesus, and then, after that, a continued pressing into shame-and-sin-eradication through exposure, confession, repentance, forgiveness, and another dose of the Gospel. Only Jesus will fix past harms. It is not only dangerous, but *fatal* in our spiritual lives to believe otherwise, to believe life is found in a new campus, new semester, or a "new me." Life is found when we walk out of our sins and into life through the power of Jesus; there's no other way. Not only does He hold the key to a shameless life, He *is* the way, the truth, and the life out of shame.

It's spiritually fatal to hold to the belief that "this time" I'll get it right, and I won't have to face my sin. I'll be a new person by the grit of my teeth. It is like an unmerciful disease, and it has most certainly contaminated my life in different seasons. It has followed me from class to naps, from the dorm room to the nights out, from recruitment to sorority houses, from my family into my friendships. And it will follow me from my first day of class to my graduation, from here until death, if I do not combat it with the Gospel—the fact that my rescue is outside of myself. And yet, through the Holy Spirit, the power outside of myself comes and lives in me.

Let go of hiding, reader. You can come out. *You really can.* You can face your failures and fears and hurts and sorrows with Jesus, and hear me—*you can*

bleeding shame

leave them behind—but only through Him. He is gentle, and He is kind, and your salvation is secure because it's in His hands (John 10:28).

Jesus is so very eager to remove your shame; you just have to come out of hiding. Come to Him, all who are weary and burdened! He gives rest from your past, from yourself, from your sin. Come to the fountain, all you who thirst! He is living water, quenching your undying need for approval and hope.

I don't think it's a coincidence that Jesus used a bleeding woman to illustrate one of the most intimate ways He turns shame into abundant life. Bleeding is so intimate, alarming, and raw. I remember the first time I heard the story of the bloody woman. It nudged my soul in a deep, untouched place, much like her own. Tears watered my cheeks and tickled my neck, my nose involuntarily snotted, and I couldn't quite put into words the heavy place where this story softly pinched my soul.

In Luke's account of this story, Jesus was headed to some serious business: to protect a young girl from death.

Yet, a desperate woman pushed through the crowd, aching, in the most literal sense, to touch the one who had healed many a hopeless cause. This sickly woman had been "bleeding" for twelve years, and many scholars agree this was a reference to her period.

(*Women reading this: can you imagine?* Twelve years of cramps, of sticky blood between your worn legs, no pads or tampons to ease the flow, no medication for the nausea and bloating, no caffeine for the accompanying weariness, no iron supplements for the light-headedness.)

This woman was likely a bloody mess, rust-colored stains on her stola, and that was not the worst of it. The worst of it does not exist in modern-day, but for this ancient woman, the public shame was the crown of her pain, the salt in her wound, as Jewish law would have classified her as unclean because of her condition. This meant she was destined to never feel the brush of a human hand, never be hugged by a loved one, never receive a handshake, never be held, never have her tears wiped away; she'd forever live on the outskirts of town until she was healed.

This was a woman who literally wore her shame, and after *twelve years* of trying to fix it herself, years of research, years of asking others, even professionals, to fix her, her condition only worsened. The sickness was rampant, and the bleeding flowed more intensely.

After years of lost hope, years of relying on human wisdom and coming up short, years of fear and trembling turning into bitterness and numbness, she pushed her way through the crowd, touching everyone she had to in order to get her hands on Jesus. She had a sense that this "Messiah" (as they called Him) was her last chance, her only chance. She took that fear and trembling to the hem of His garment.

And with one trusting, desperate moment of belief, the woman who was not allowed to touch anyone because of her dirtiness...touched the Savior.

Instant healing.

She heard the voice of her Savior, her Rescuer saying, "Daughter, your faith made you *well*."

Only a little while later, He did continue on His mission and raised that little girl from the dead, but that little girl was not the only one who Jesus brought back to life again that day in Gerasenes. After all the striving, searching other places for a fix, other places for healing, her remedy was found in Jesus Christ, Son of the living God, our ultimate Healer.

I've listened to the mantras that millennials are prescribed when dealing with crippling shame. The "I am enough," "You just need more self-confidence," "If you got it, flaunt it," the numbing and escapism, the suppressing and hiding of our true hurts, the "I'll get it right this time around."

These mottos are worthless, honestly. They assume a solution is within ourselves, forgetting that it is just as broken as the rest of us.

They just made me bleed more.

Shame tells us we can do it ourselves, no one else struggles as we do, no one really needs to know the real us, that Jesus would turn away if He really knew who we are, our problem is that we aren't good enough. Our culture tells us we are the solution to our own problem.

bleeding shame

I think maybe our problem is that you and I don't believe how good *He* is.

Oh, college students, He *knows* every detail of our shames anyway—the memories we suppress the most, the places we want to numb, the things that make us cry alone in the communal bathroom stalls, the sin we just can't seem to get under control, the words we can't utter even when we are alone, the words that cause us to wince in pain, the things we did to hurt another person, the specific words that cut us to the core that we suppress on an hourly basis.

And He is inviting us to bring them to Him—to let Him *heal* those things.

Don't worry about bringing your mess to Jesus. He fixes, cleanses, and heals. Unlike everyone else she touched and caused to be "unclean," when she reached for Jesus, the woman did not make Him dirty. No, through her believing touch, Jesus made her *clean*. That's the power of our Savior. He is the solution to our mess.

When we come to Him with our blood, we do not stain Him—He cleans us.

When we come to Him with our wounds, He makes us new.

When we come with our darkness, He gives us light.

When we come with our shame, He makes us pure.

Confessing sin and shame is not something we grow out of. No, just like we don't graduate from high school shames, we cannot graduate from shame as a whole either, not until Jesus comes. But as we choose to nourish our souls with the Biblical truth of Christ instead of toxifying them with lies from the world, we will see that, in time, Jesus really does make true on His promise to heal us, pulling us out of darkness and into light. As we believe in Him, we can watch Him knock down our high walls and fill in our gaps with love.

I apologize for the over-use of the word "shame." I tried to find other words to describe the feeling, and none of them were quite right or had quite the helpless, soul-taking connotation that word does. I have a suspicion that the reason we don't have many words for "shame" is because we don't talk about it enough to invent new words because we are too afraid of its power.

contemplations of a collegiate christian

Too bad for shame. It doesn't know Christ is seated on the throne and it is not. And my deepest regrets are the days I have spent believing and living like it was the opposite.

I'm done spending any more days like that—hiding and afraid.

I'm finished picking up what He has asked me to put down.

I'm finished holding on to things He has already let go.

I'm done with darkness. I'm ready for light.

TEN

close proximity

Tranquility hides in small spaces.
Diane Ackerman

The living space of the Lighthouse was fairly roomy, but with six girls, it was forever crowded.

We called the extra bathroom off the kitchen the "boys bathroom," where we hung up all our clothes to dry because the drying rack was almost always full. We had a cute laundry room with a string pull-light, where I could almost guarantee that, when you most needed to wash your underwear, the washer and dryer would already be loaded.

Sara Beth and I shared the room on the top right, where we giggled and talked ourselves to sleep at times and ignored the fact that everyone could hear every word of our FaceTime dates with our boyfriends.

You could hear a pin drop from the farthest corners of the house, like it was right next to your ear. Our driveway flooded every time it rained a half-inch, cockroaches and spiders became our uninvited roommates, and ants were constantly letting themselves in without even knocking.

Kitchens made for three people get small when six bodies are trying to fit. There was hardly a moment to make dinner alone, and bumping booties and "excuse me's" were constants.

Our driveway was practically a parking lot, fitting about nine cars with a tight squeeze.

contemplations of a collegiate christian

With a flameless fireplace and college budgets to cover the utility bill, the winter was cold, but our rituals brought warm spirits. Blankets were folded over every corner of every piece of furniture, and no blanket discrimination was allowed in our home—fuzzy dollar-store Disney characters and grandma's gorgeous handmade quilts were equals in the Lighthouse. The bookshelves and side tables were always filled with mugs of steaming tea, and if you were on a tight budget, plain hot water would do the job just fine.

The Lighthouse turned into a lake house during rainy weeks, our driveway having no effective draining system. I giggled a thousand times watching from the window seat as my roommates moved like gymnast-ninjas to avoid the knee-deep puddles and finally surrendered to wet socks. I was also the gymnast-ninja at times, which was laughable when I gave myself over fully to the role.

About 18,394 screams were screeched as cockroaches exposed themselves right before bedtime, to which we all found ourselves breathing heavily and hugging one another as the bravest of the bunch (always Amber or Kendra) whacked at them with the nearest shoe, rolling their eyes at our hysteria.

I had to learn how to deal with interruptions in the Lighthouse. Thin walls, big bugs, and small budgets brought more chaos than I would have preferred. However, if anything, the Lighthouse taught me that interruptions and these small hardships were hardly inconveniences, and inconveniences often awaken us to the most important things.

There were winter nights when I would rather the thermostat be higher, but snuggle sessions warmed my heart.

There were summer days when I would rather cockroaches be non-existent, but their presence called laughter into existence.

There were days when I didn't want to do my roommate's dirty dishes, but the repetitive action was a time for prayer.

Interruptions and inconveniences often bring me back to who I am, Whose I am, to where I want to be, to the closeness we are all longing for in the first place. They interject to face my irritable wrath, by stopping me from my hurried life, eventually calming me and grounding me in the reality that love cannot always be scheduled or planned for. They offer themselves as an opportunity to let go of my own plan for my time, and rise to the occasion that I'm met with. Road-blocks cause me to embrace the situations, rather than fight them.

The Lighthouse taught me the lesson that no matter our preferences and pleas, love will not yield to our calendars, but our calendars, plans, schedules, and desires must yield to love. This order cannot and should not be reversed.

Submitting to love doesn't look like never having anything on your calendar, never having a plan for the day and leaving it up to "fate," never setting up boundaries, never saying "no" to someone, or always being available. That's a cheap version of "love."

But it does mean that, when met with a situation that needs attention, we don't consider it an interruption of our original plans. We consider it an opportunity to represent Christ's love.

We live in a world that elevates our own space and independence, idolizing self and rejecting servanthood. You don't bother me, and I won't bother you. You watch Netflix on your phone, and I'll watch the show I want to watch on my phone. A queen bed is better than a full, a bigger house better than a smaller one, thicker walls better than thinner, order-your-own individualized dinner rather than choosing and cooking a meal together. We love autonomy and despise sacrifice.

But living so near to others forced me into situations and moments I wouldn't trade for the world; conviction about my own selfishness and moments to love that I would have never experienced living alone.

Love is better and bigger and wider than myself, and community is better than isolation, even when it's inconvenient.

I love my space at times; don't get me wrong. I need my alone time, just like we all do. There's nothing wrong with that. Give yourself that space, in order to fuel your brain and your heart and your soul. Jesus retreated. We all need retreat at times.

But I've had seasons where I held a little too tightly to my "me" time, and I think I've begun to understand that the truest form, the highest form of love often grows in tight spaces, in nearness, in close proximity.

ELEVEN

the treadmill

"Why do you spend money on that which is not bread, and your labor on that which does not satisfy? Listen, listen to me, and eat what is good, and you will delight in the richest of fare. Give ear and come to me; listen, that you may live. I will make an everlasting covenant with you, my faithful love promised to David."

The Lord, Isaiah 55:2-3, ESV

Sometimes I really hate the way I enter my home from a day of lab work and classes on campus: tired, a little dazed, blind to important and heart-filling things, numbed to spiritual things, meaninglessly adding to my to-do list, and simultaneously longing to mark off the next thing.

The issue is not the classes or the lab work or the to-do list— it's that I love the earthly labor too much. I love it so much, in fact, I have too often served it as my master, letting interesting theories, a clear checklist, endless articles, a clean room, and books of scientific information steal time from what my soul really longs for: intimacy with its Maker. Prayer time and retreating with God slip to the side when I let the tasks pile beyond what my human brain and body were meant for.

As much as I wish this habit was not so broken and my heart not so much of an idol factory, too often my to-do list sits on the throne while retreating with God comes at the bottom on my list of priorities, right behind working out and making my bed. Too often, I have served cognitive psychology or my school newspaper with more fervor, more exhilaration, more excitement than I have served the One through whom cognition and history have their existence.

contemplations of a collegiate christian

As I exchange necessary intimacy with the Source of Life for a quick study session, for writing another newspaper article for my job, or for catching up with the friend that I just saw yesterday, I unconsciously imagine that adding one more thing to my "what-I-did-today" list will fill me up. Scripture attests that work is good, commendable, and does well for both the spirit and the flesh. It says that it's satisfying in portion, but there is a threshold to its satisfaction. After some point, the longer the list gets, the emptier my soul becomes.

It's funny how my soul still falls into the trap over and over again, but I have not learned to recognize this trap until now, this allurement of "the grind" as our culture so fondly calls it. Sure, I knew people struggled with prioritizing the most important things, but I never really thought of that as an area where I struggled.

I never miss worship on Sundays or my campus ministry retreats; I love them too much! I would think to myself, not recognizing that I often shoved personal time in prayer aside just to check off another thing from my to-do list. I thought this was the same as sitting in His presence. "Where two or more are gathered," right? Though I did often gather with many in His name, I had forgotten all of the times when Jesus retreated to be alone with the Father to pray, and it was so often when the busyness was at its peak.

I was so good at deceiving myself into believing I was spending time with God, I would often busy myself reading theological articles, meeting with people in the Church, and ministering to unbelievers. How could I be missing intimacy with Him? All the labor seems pretty intimate. It's a tricky and deceiving place to be, and I easily forget what His presence feels like whenever I prioritize earthly, frantic labor over His calming nearness.

God has shown me in the last season that my heart is always tricking itself, always deceiving itself that I am somehow superhuman, that somehow God was not addressing me when He was addressing all of humanity in the Bible clearly stating we should rest every seventh day, that we are limited and not limitless, that our hearts will constantly wander, and that we should question our motives constantly because He should be first, first, first—always first. And without Him being first, we find ourselves ruined: overworked, bone-tired, bitter, desperately weary, and *still* dissatisfied.

the treadmill

We convince ourselves we aren't all of these lifeless things, that this hard labor, this chasing after the wind, this "grind" is a good life.

He often lets me run after the wind for a while, letting me frustrate my limits. Soon enough, I become tired and hungry, as He disciplines me by allowing me to feel the emptiness once again.

This endless work is like a treadmill—never stopping, leading nowhere but weariness. In His grace, He eventually unplugs the deceiving, laborious treadmill I have fashioned for myself.

What happens when He unplugs it is usually this: I will be forced to stop running. Dazed, confused, and dizzy from the halt, I will step off. I will go look at the plug, trying to see what went wrong with the outlet, why it isn't providing purpose anymore, and I will search for my lost busyness-exhilaration among the wires. After a while, I will eventually retreat to the floor, butt on the ground, elbows on knees, head between legs, exhaling loudly. I will stare at the treadmill for one more moment, hoping it will magically start back up and my work will be revived. *One more thing to do, please?* When it doesn't, I close my eyes, let some tears fall, and plead to God to come and meet me here by this broken treadmill, to revive my confused, frustrated, and weary heart. All the running has me dazed, confused, and I have forgotten my true purpose was not to perform but to enjoy Him. In His ultimate humility and commitment to sweaty and stinky sinners like me, He will meet me still. Just like in James 4:8* He keeps His promise of intangible intimacy, no matter what my record looks like.

After a long discussion, themed with confusion about where I went wrong, He will expose my heart to myself. I will look in the mirror and see the reality of my idolatry's depth—my unbelief that He is enough. Remorse will lead to confession, confession to repentance, repentance to the story of a God-man who executed my sins thousands of years ago, that murder scene to a resurrection, and that sweet Gospel to ultimate and eternal comfort.

I will be reminded, for the thousandth time, that wind is uncatchable, and only the Bread of Life fills me up.

---

* *"Come close to God, and God will come close to you. Wash your hands, you sinners; purify your hearts, for your loyalty is divided between God and the world." (NLT)*

contemplations of a collegiate christian

I will weep shameful and sticky tears, but He will not be ashamed of me. I will snuggle the moment, let Him wrap my sweaty and weary soul in His loving kindness that was there all along, waiting for me to step off the treadmill, look Him in the face, and see abundant Life for what He really is.

I will open my eyes, and the treadmill will look much different—much less appealing, much more empty, and I will wonder why I thought a machine that leads to nowhere was so enticing in the first place. The more this pattern of redemption repeats itself, the more I see its necessity.

I know there will be seasons that, slowly and connivingly, I will convince myself it won't hurt to tip-toe back on the treadmill for a minute and test it out. I will fall back into self-deception again, I'm sure, but hopefully, the more I repeat this cycle, the less often it will happen. That seems to be the pattern of sanctification.

I will test His limits at times. He will allow it, knowing without Him, I will ultimately break a bone, skin my knees, fall flat on my face, and He will come to sweetly and graciously rescue me from myself once again.

However, until then, I'm doing all I can to stay right here in His embrace, staring at the treadmill, and searching for the scissors to cut its cord.

TWELVE

nothing less than friend-zoned

"I could easily forgive his pride, if he had not mortified mine."
Elizabeth Bennett, *Pride and Prejudice*

Dating. It's stressful and exciting. It's terrible and wonderful. It's heart-lifting and heart-breaking. And everyone, it seems, is attracted to the paradox. Almost everyone wants to do it.

It seems whenever numbers are low at college ministry, the thing to do is a series on romance, and people come out of the woodwork. Since the beginning, in the Garden of Eden, we've been wired for relationships (as your campus minister will point out in this series), so it makes sense. And the ultimate human relationship is marriage. This process, if you will, is talked about in the terms of the romantic progression: single, dating, engaged, married.

Dating seems to be the one people are the most anxious to hear about. They want to hear the *rules*. Like when to call, when to text, when and how to ask on a date. And, does she think I'm weird? Am I overdressed? Do I really want him to see me without doing my makeup first? And, what if I'm not attracted to their body, you know? Isn't that important? And, what if we are really attracted, maybe *too* attracted—what then?

As a married person, I've gone through all the phases completely now. Even though I know there are a million people trying to give you advice on the how-to's and such, I want to give just a few of my thoughts on the dating process. Take them for what they are worth, test them against wisdom, but there are four things I really want everyone to know about the second stage called dating:

First, **dating is way more similar to friendship than you might think, and** *it's awesome.*

Being friend-zoned isn't that far from dating, and dating isn't that far from being friend-zoned, from my experience. I think the status of "dating" could even be compared to an intentional friendship between a man and a woman. The only difference between the "not dating" and the "dating" in guy-and-girl friendship is the intentionality behind it, with the intention being an evaluation of a life-long commitment to marriage and romance.

Dating can be awesome, especially when pressing into the freedom of friend-ship! Friendship isn't a limitation; it's actually an invitation. You don't have to hide all the parts of yourself to make yourself appear more desirable to the other sex. You are just friends. You discuss your passions and hobbies, your fears and hopes, your testimonies, your theology, your plans for the future, your favorite movies and blogs, and everything else you discuss with a friend.

And then you seek wisdom, through counsel, prayer, and the Word, whether this would be a good fit for your spouse.

Dating is so fun when it's like hanging out with your friend, learning about them, laughing with them, talking about God with them, dreaming with them, and just doing life together. Friendship is amazing, and dating isn't that far from it, just with a specific evaluation for the relationship beyond just friendship.

Secondly, a thing I've heard a lot lately is the idea "you don't owe each other anything." And I'm here to say, in the gentlest way, ***that's not true***.

I've heard this quite a few times, in quite a few discussions on dating, and I just want to say I don't really think it's 100% accurate, and though it might be well-intended, is misleading.

This statement was said for the sake of those who think that their boyfriend or girlfriend owes the other their time, body, money, etc. It's a reactionary state-ment, and it should be understood within that context. And it's true: they don't technically owe you any of that. You don't owe each other your bodies, in any way, shape, or form. (And you should be seeking purity and holiness above all else for one another.) You don't owe each other time, and you shouldn't expect an "I love you" or any sort of commitment during the dating season, beyond intentional friendship. In fact, you need to be super-duper careful with these treasured words, actions, and affections. Guard and keep them safe! Don't throw them around. You actually don't owe each other your romantic affection or love, believe it or not. These are valuable and powerful, and no, we don't owe each other these things. We must use extreme discretion when it comes to these things because they are of such value, much like a new car or a diamond ring.

However, that's not the end of the story, and "you don't owe them anything" was meant for a certain context of people who thought the person they were dating owed them something like their body, time, money, etc.

If the attitude is simply "I don't owe you anything," what type of relationship is that? Do you have any other good relationships that are founded on that attitude? I don't. If I treated my friends with the approach "I don't owe you anything; you don't owe me anything," what type of relationship would that be?

No; I think the heart attitude we are called to is something entirely different. It is unlike "I don't owe you anything" or "You owe me something," both of which are attitudes of the world.

Though you don't owe each other those things, I mentioned earlier, you *do* owe each other another type of attitude that is wonderful, edifying, selfless, caring; one which is grounded in this idea of friendship. This is an attitude of Jesus, who cared for His neighbors, who lavished kindness, who acted indebted to those who were indebted to Him.

The heart attitude is one of honor.

The Bible calls us to "outdo one another in showing honor" (Romans 12:10, ESV). You *do* owe each other kindness. You *do* owe each other closure instead of "ghosting." You *do* owe each other forgiveness. You *do* owe each other honesty. You *do* owe each other respect for your bodies. You *do* owe each other any space needed to feed undivided devotion to the Lord.

You don't owe each other anything more than friendship, this is true—but you don't owe each other anything less either. To act as if friendship is less than kind, courteous, caring, attentive, loving, and intentional is wrong and unbiblical. Friends lookout for the other's best. Friends are committed to one another's sanctification. Friends sacrifice their pride for the sake of one another. Friends are honest. Friends are gentle. Friends care for one another.

In dating, just like friendship, you are bound to each other as friends, and friends don't act with an attitude of "I don't owe you anything."

Friends are kinder than that.

Dating can be a sweet and wonderful thing, no matter how it turns out, if you choose to see each other and treat each other like friends, nothing less. Act like servants of the Lord, like brother and sister to each other. Treat each other like you care about their bodies enough not to intrude on them, their time enough to honor it, their conscience enough not to compromise it, their heart enough not to fiddle with it, their sanctification enough to fuel it.

So, no; you don't owe each other your bodies; you owe each other caring enough about their bodies to stir them towards Christ's intention for their bodies.

No; you don't owe each other your time; you owe each other respect of their time.

No; you don't owe each other romantic "I love you's"; you owe each other care and friendly affection, honesty, and protection for one another's hearts, no matter how you individually decide that plays out in your relationship.

And maybe you differ about what you think these things mean. Maybe you think caring for each other's time requires a two-hour phone call a day, and he doesn't. Or maybe you think caring for each other's bodies is never kissing before the wedding day, and she doesn't. Maybe it's a big enough deal to each of you that you decide to part ways in this dance of dating.

If that happens, you know what? You owe each other the friendly kindness of letting each other go and moving on.

So maybe this… what if we shifted from the dating attitude of "I don't owe you _____/ you don't owe me_____" to "I care about you enough that I think the best decision is _____."

There might not technically even be much change in action, but there's a change of heart attitude, and that affects everything.

nothing less than friend-zoned

I think our dating relationships would already look more kind and gentle, maybe cause a little less pain if we recognized that they were nothing less than friendship, and God holds friendship in high regard.

Dating my husband was so wonderful, so life-giving, and so *fun* because we had these servant-minded attitudes of a deep obligation to the other's best and deep respect for the image of God in the other person, in their heart, mind, body, conscience, and soul.

I want that for each of you if dating looks like something you want to do.

The third thing I want you to know: **romantic situations are very individual, so you are going to have to do the hard work of prayer and wisdom-seeking if you want to have guidance for your particular situation.**

I wanted the formula when I was dating. I wanted the rules. He says this; I do this. He makes this move; I make that one. Rules were safe; blurred lines, hearing the Holy Spirit's guidance, and making wisdom-based moves seemed risky.

But that's not how dating works; it's not how relationships work. You don't have hard rules when it comes to friendships and coffee dates. There aren't even super hard-and-fast rules in the business or professional world at times. These relationships require risks, and luckily, we have a Father who wants to offer all the wisdom we need (James 1:5).

And since the nature of romantic relationships is so situational and personal, much more than that of a business relationship, they require a lot of wisdom.

There are only two things I've found as constants: You should date someone who shares your Christian faith and convictions, and someone you enjoy being around.

The rest is revealed through prayer, the Word, the Spirit, and wisdom. You will take risks. You will ask questions, and you will get hurt at times. That's how any type of relationship works, and though you might get wounded, dating is worth it when you walk by the Spirit and respect the other person, and they do the same for you.

And they can turn out to have the most positive end... marriage!
The last thing is... **it might be someone you never expected**.

Allow me to tell you the story about my sweet husband, Kyle Schumpert. We met at a book study through our campus ministry, and Kyle, a junior at the time, was very annoyed that freshman girls (like me) were coming to the book study. I thought "the guy with the beard" was probably a jerk, and I was consequently very annoyed whenever he said wise things during the Bible study.

We both, unknowingly, had a deep passion for quality guacamole, which eventually brought us to the beginning of our friendship: the Guac-Off. This friendly guacamole competition turned into another, Guac-Off 2.0 (which, I won, by the way), which led to a Guac Party, which all led to deeper friendship, good discussion about the Gospel, and lots of laughter.

Soon enough, God put it on both of our hearts that we wanted to know each other more, and through many coffee house dates, book store visits, chess games, shared podcasts, long phone calls, and much prayer, we grew closer and closer. There were bumps in the road, as we both evaluated our dreams for life and our desire for one another, but we eventually decided we didn't want a life without each other.

However, if you had told me during my freshman year I would marry Kyle Schumpert, I would have never believed you. Kyle Schumpert? What? No way. I even legendarily once told my friend, "Kyle Schumpert would never find himself a girlfriend, much less a WIFE!" (This in a dumb moment of anger because he joked with me and embarrassed me.)

Look at me now—his wife, and I couldn't be happier about it. I love that man deeply.

Dating, like friendship and all relationships, is messy but has the potential to be beautiful and rewarding. It can end in good stories, and it can transition into a life-long relationship. I am so grateful for the time I spent dating my husband, and even for the few, short dating relationships I had before him. Would I go back and date those men? Probably not, but I don't hold any hard feelings, and I do have some funny stories about my journey to finding Kyle.

So, it turns out that dating (and hopefully finding your spouse, if you so desire) isn't quite *that* far from being friend-zoned; the only difference (though, important) is an acknowledgment of the intentionality behind the relationship.

So treat each other kindly, outdo one another in honor, love, and respect.

And don't be so afraid of being friend-zoned.

After all, it isn't that far from dating.

THIRTEEN

more than a trophy

"This is my beloved, and this is my friend"
King Solomon, Song of Solomon 5:16, ESV

So, you've found them, the one whom your soul loves, your best friend. The person who you laugh and cry with. The person with whom you have shared in sanctification and conviction. The person you pull closer when their sin weighs them down, you call each other out of darkness and into the light. The person you choose to hang out with on the nothing-to-do Saturdays, and the person you choose to talk to on the phone for hours on the too-busy-to-do-anything-but-work days.

This is the person. Your person.

And now, it's time. You have arrived at the season of speculation. When are we going to talk about "it"? Will he just skip that, get down on one knee, and ask the question? You spend late nights speculating the weekends he could do it, listen for any subtle hints.

Engagement, maybe? Holy matrimony, anyone?

It's a sweet, wonderful time. A cherished and heart-beating-fast season; so scary because it's so important. You are slightly obsessed with the thought of him getting down on one knee, and you can't quite believe it's happening, because *WHEN DID WE GET THIS OLD WHERE WE ARE THE ENGAGED*

---

* *They are not technically "yours." You are not married. "Yours" here = the person who you just enjoy being with, have the same vision as, etc. And vice versa.*

AND MARRIED ONES?

It's thrilling, and I've lived through it personally with Kyle and vicariously through my friends. I got engaged in the fall of my senior year, and I was married a month before graduation. One of my best friends got engaged over that Christmas break, and we stood beside another best friend on her wedding day a week later. My other good friend's wedding was at the beginning of our senior year, and she was pregnant a couple of months later.

But as sweet as the season of engagement and marriage may be, I've seen the ugly side of it that the world has twisted into two things it was never meant to be: an achievement and a burden.

On one side of the equation, I had many girls come up to me, squealing and excitedly wanting to see "THE RING!!!!" They noted how shiny it was, how he did such a good job, how I was so lucky. I agreed with all these things, smiling excitedly. But then, I got a pat on the back for getting the "ring before spring," and I realized she thought the moment was more of a performance than a moment between two people who love one another, that my ring was more of a trophy than a promise.

My heart hurt. I wanted to tell her it wasn't a trophy, and his proposal wasn't a performance. It was so much more than the (grainy) photographs. That moment was a beautiful, risky, and wonderful question, followed by a promise to make a covenant together.

On the other side, I've also had friends who have been judged for their engagement or getting married before they graduated. I've heard the prideful and snide comments, people laughing because they were "too focused on their career for marriage," as if getting married means you no longer have aspirations or goals outside of your covenant, as if marriage is a second priority to career, nothing more than a one-way ticket into the kitchen and laundry room, and as if cooking and laundry weren't as important as "real work."* I've been told so often "but you're *too young* to get married!" as if marriage was a cage I was locking myself inside or the suicide of my happiness.**

As if those things won't have to be done anyway...
** And then I want to ask, "Would you rather have fewer years with your spouse than more?"

more than a trophy

The thing is this, both sides get it wrong: marriage is neither a validation of my importance as a human being nor is it a burden to be carried.

Both perspectives make marriage out to be something different than it is. To the world, it is either an achievement (not a promise) or it is simply a duty (not a privilege and joy).

Marriage is this: a covenant between woman and a man to love each other more than anything or anyone else besides God Himself, to give of oneself for the other in body, soul, spirit, and mind, to never leave or forsake this commitment, to call each other into holiness as they walk in the light of the Gospel, for all their Earthly days.

This is marriage; nothing less or more. It's perfect in this design because it's based on how we are designed: God is our priority, next is our romantic human relationship, next is our children, next everything else.

I pray this for those of us who are in the Church. May we show the world, and maybe even understand ourselves, marriage was God's idea and gift to us. It was a good thing when Eve was given to Adam, for both of them. Marriage is not a trophy; it's a covenant relationship. Marriage is not simply a responsibility; it is a privilege and a gift.

Don't give in to the lie that, if you are to get married in college or your early twenties, you are settling for a less-than life. Also don't give in to the lie that you finally "made it" because you will have the title of wife or husband. Don't make marriage more or less than what it is. It is a covenant relationship, a joy—just like the covenant relationship between Christ and His bride is a joy.

That spring day, on March 21, 2020, my husband and I promised to love one another, to never forsake one another, to honor and cherish, no matter what life brought us, in all seasons, forever.

That promise is nothing less than a beautiful covenant, an honor, a privilege.

Thank God engagement rings are not trophies, and marriage is far from a burden.

FOURTEEN

college cliques

"When we do the hard, intimate work of friendship,
we bring a little more of the divine into daily life."
Shauna Niequist

They say you never grow out of high school, right? Sadly, this statement seems true because high school is just the introduction into "the real world." It makes me sad that I even have to write this chapter, but it's the facts, and one of the most requested topics I cover in this book. I feel like by college, we should be past the "in" and "out" crowd conversation. We should at least be over the "he said" and "she said" talk. However, like I mentioned in chapters prior, I'm learning that maturity is not the product of age; it's the product of choice.

So, cliques must be addressed because they *do* exist in college and beyond. Maybe even more surprisingly, they function the same way they did in high school. The only difference is they usually don't seem quite as weighty later in life, simply because there are often many more people to choose from. In high school, there were only a few hundred people, so you had to face the cliques every day in classes, in the cafeteria, and down the hallways. If you go to a de-cent-sized college, there are many more fish in your sea of campus, so cliques are avoidable, and the reminder of your non-membership in their group isn't a constant like it was in your high school cafeteria.

However, though they are less looming, cliques and their accompanying hurt still exists in college.

Now, it isn't bad to have a group of friends to form a community with—not at all. But there are healthy and unhealthy groups, and I think this is the distinction between cliques and friendships.

Cliques thrive on fear. Whether it's the subtle fear of exclusivity, the fear of being counted out, or the fear you won't be enough for them, fear is their foundation. Cliques don't do much without each other, and FOMO* often fuels the large attendance at spontaneous group hang-outs. They have inside jokes, and they don't really want to let you in on them, secretly priding themselves on the fact that outsiders don't know the joke or the story. They don't want others in their group, and if they do allow someone in, that person has to be especially cool or earn the right to be there. They make a chat group and don't want other people added. They are sure to constantly bring up "the group." They have opinions about who should and shouldn't be included. They know it isn't actually cool to be *known* as exclusive, so they exclude people in subtle and sneaky ways, like "forgetting" to add someone in the group message or avoiding conversation with that person in public. They will charm you by complimenting you, but there is no real feeling of safety or love within the friend group as a whole—only this subtle sense that if I am not funny, attractive, popular, smart, hipster, political, rich, sometimes even "unique" enough, then I'm not going to belong. If I miss any hang outs, stories, or events, then I'll be counted out. I won't be worthy. I have to earn my place here, either through my economy of attendance, attractiveness, popularity, comedy, or likeability. Cliques are insecure and fragile, and you will always feel this unrest in your soul, like you are running a treadmill to be included.

Friend groups are different; they thrive on love, the type that drives out fear (1 John 4:18). Friend groups aren't fragile; they are life-giving and healthy. No one is taking names about who is in and who is out, and you don't have to bring your resume of likeability to your hang-outs. You don't have to be on your best game or look your best when you're with them. They naturally erupt out of genuine interest and love for one another. No one is keeping score here, so you aren't shamed if you aren't going to the event this Friday with everyone else; they just wish you could be there with them. They seek out your presence because they simply enjoy you. If you are out of town this weekend, they will likely invite you to coffee next week so y'all can catch up because they miss you and want to hear how you're doing. They know you've been busy. They like seeing you happy, healthy, and thriving, and they want what's best for you.

---

* *Fear of missing out*

They aren't trying to charm you into liking them; they will tell you the hard truths when you need to be told (Proverbs 27:6). You are more than someone they enjoy; you are someone they love. You aren't a threat to their status or their inclusion. You aren't being measured up based on what you offer; you are a human they are here to love. Sure, you have inside jokes, and sometimes you don't want to explain them to others, but that's because they are embarrassing or they won't think it's as funny as you do—not because you don't want them to be included.

Friend groups aren't trying to build a wall or push anyone out, though they allow you space when necessary. No one is taking tallies, and if you were at some point, there was a moment when you realized you didn't have to do that anymore. You can rest here in friendship. You can let others rest here too. You can be loved here, and you can extend love here. No punches will be pulled. Fear isn't constantly crouching at your door. Stay for a while, leave early, you're loved just the same. Breathe in, breathe out—these are your *friends*, closer than brothers, committed like sisters. Brothers don't walk out because they had a boring or hard day together. They stick it out. So, you can put down the resume and the mask. You don't have to fight to be here.

I've been in both the cliques and the friend groups. In cliques, I've experienced both the sting of rejection and the excitement of approval. They may seem fun for a while until you're the one on the outside looking in, until you see someone you care about get hurt, until you get tired of the treadmill and start wondering why you have to clean up every time you hang out with friends, until you realize this is fragile and surface-level and your soul is longing for more.

And then, when you choose to walk away, the friends are there. They are there when you've been hurt by your desire to be popular. They are there when you are hurt by your own sin. They are there to meet you when you've abandoned them. They are there for you, committed to your holiness, committed to your brotherhood in Christ, committed to *you*, in spite of it all.

Friendship is sweeter, kinder, and eternal. Cliques are restless, hurtful, and temporary.

There will always be blurred lines. Friend groups might have clique-ish tendencies. Some cliques might be more friendly than others. However, the goal is to strive for friends over cliques.

So, how to strive for friendships instead of clique-ships? To have friends, you need to be a friend. Friendship is a two-way street. Both people have to let go of their frantic desire to be constantly approved of and applauded for. You have to let down your guard, let people love you in your mess. The other person has to let others let down their guard, and you need to love them fiercely, speaking both truth and grace, in their messiest times.

Jesus wasn't about cliques. (Though it seems like the religiously prideful probably were.) He made room for anyone who truly wanted to be with Him (John 14:2). He came to be a friend to the friendless, to the people who got kicked to the curb because they didn't measure up to the cliques of the Pharisee's religion or worldly standards of "righteousness." He came for the hurting and broken who needed a place to finally rest secure, free of the proving and fighting.

I hope we can dive into true friendship, the most authentic and live-giving kind. I have spent time in cliques, and they were always a waste of my valuable energy and emotions.

Cliques are temporary, and they will fade or stab each other in the back.

True friendships will last. They are eternal.

Use your college years to establish some eternal friendships.

FIFTEEN

more than cozy

"Beware the Instagram Bible, my daughters – those filtered frames festooned with feathered verses, adorned in all manner of loops and tails, bedecked with blossoms, saturated with sunsets, culled and curated just for you. Beware lest it become for you your source of daily bread. It is telling a partial truth."

Jen Wilkin

It's really funny how, for some reason, I find myself trying to re-create the "Instagram Bible" moments in my own time with God. I don't even do it consciously. My intention is to simply sit with the Lord, but then something overtakes me, and instead of pulling out my Bible and prayer journal, I turn on my essential oils diffuser and open my curtains for good lighting. Next, I search for the perfect pen that writes flawlessly, start the kettle to pour a cup of tea, clear off my clean desk for an even tidier surface, open my journal and subconsciously critique my handwriting as I write the date, like a calligraphy warm-up of sorts. Fifteen minutes or so pass me by, and I haven't even opened Scripture yet.

I didn't mean to end up here, fluffing up my time with the Lord. I guess somewhere along the way, I accidentally bought into the message this was how meeting with God always went: candles, coffee, calligraphy, cozy...and then, of course, after all of these staples, I could add the Bible and prayer!

Yet, what I'm learning is this: although I do meet God sometimes with candles, essential oils, elegant handwriting, and whatnot, I meet God just as intensely in the uncomfortable, messy moments, stripped of candles and coffee. I'm talking lay-over-at-the-airport, bad-breath, and bags-under-eyes kind of meet up. On days when I am the most hopeless and most worn, I crawl to His Word, and I find it to be the most satisfying. It becomes water for my parched soul, rest for my weariness, beauty in my brokenness, even when it's void of aesthetics.

He longs to meet me in my messy, non-Instagram-worthy moments.

"But first, Jesus" is the anthem of many Instagram Christian girls. But if I were to be honest, my actions too often have said, *"But first, candles, coffee, calligraphy, comfortable and pretty and cozy things...and then Jesus."*

I'm finding this type of setup is reflective of a heart issue I picked up along the way, one that is more harmful than it is helpful. I'm not saying there's anything wrong with the "c's" (candles, coffee, calligraphy, comfortable and cozy) necessarily. I do love these beautiful moments with leather-bound books, the Bible, good smells, and warm lighting. However, if I am convinced God is less here because I don't look like an Instagram star, there's a problem.

Though my time is by no means *less* holy if I have such an atmosphere, the c's definitely don't make my time *more* holy. Essential oils and golden lighting don't elevate my absorption of God's Word.

I often act like I need to prepare for a tea party before I come to Jesus. Sure, He loves tidy me, but if I'm being candid, during college, these moments weren't reflective of who I was most days. Tidy me is not my norm, and Jesus is trying to meet me in my beautiful *and* my normal moments. He is happy to meet with the put-together version of Mary Mad, no doubt. She's no less of a person, worthy of love. *But* He also wants to meet with the me who has scribbles all over her left hand, twenty sticky notes on her desk, and smeared mascara on her face. He's happy to embrace the Mary Mad who just drank off-brand coffee, doesn't yet understand that Greek word, and can't always come up with a good Instagram caption. He wants to reveal Himself to this version of me just as much as He wants to reveal Himself to the me with make-up, good handwriting, who is well-rested and well-fed, calm and collected. Whoever I am that day, that's the Mary Mad God is trying to reveal Himself to, and I need to stop limiting my time spent with Him to only one version of myself.

I'm done requiring my space to be cozy and my person to be tidy in order to meet with God. There's nothing wrong with cozy—in fact, we have a God of comfort, for sure. However, He is also the God who gets His hands dirty in my mess, too, in order to bring me *true* comfort. He has the kind of comfort that isn't situational; it doesn't depend on my environment. He meets me in the well-ordered moments with comfort, and He meets me in my mess with comfort. He will meet me at any moment, and I've got to stop acting like a scented candle ignites His presence.

He did tell many a scared Israelite to "fear not"—in the midst of great distress. He told His people of His forgiveness—at the altar, with death and blood and guts, in the repercussions of their sin and fallenness. He discipled His friends—in the middle of stinky fish boats and crashing waves. He gave a blind man sight—by rubbing spit and dirt on His eyes. He spoke love into the adulterous woman's life—when she lay in the dirt, tear-stained, likely naked. All these moments were the process of God meeting with His people, calling out to them, inviting them to Himself, in the middle of their messes. We can most understand His strength when we are at our weakness, His purity when we are most dirty, His grace when we are our most sinful.

All of this shows me—yes—God can meet me here, with my ugly mugs and fluorescent lighting.

This might seem a small thing to you like I'm being petty about the Instagram Christian stereotype, but I think the physical reality can truly affect the spiritual if we aren't careful. The culture of the screen has convinced me I need to come to the Lord ready for a photography session and having taken calligraphy classes. This easily transfers to me believing I have to come to God with all of the right prayers, all of the right theological training, all of the right questions even. This is dangerous territory. God isn't asking me to leave my baggage at the door; He's inviting me to bring my chaos in, and He will make order out of it.

With that said, I am proposing that calligraphy and cozy might sometimes be getting in the way of some awesomely intense, grace-filled moments.

So, here I am, declaring I'm done fixing myself up before I come to the Lord. Some days I will be more put-together. Other days, my fallenness might be more evident than I'd like. Either way, I'm coming out of pretend, coming as I am, and asking Him to change me from one degree of holiness into the next, no matter how high the degree is.

Only cozy devotional time, only warm-and-cozy Jesus, and only perfect handwriting— I'm letting go of you. You aren't a prerequisite to grace, and I'm finished believing the lie that you make my time any sweeter with God.

There are days when the essential oils just distract me from His whispering, and there isn't an oil for Bible absorption, so I'm going to take a break from them for a while. I'm also over the watercolors that have wrinkled the pages of the Psalms and pressed flowers that are constantly falling out of my Bible. I can't keep up with all of them, and I'm just a terrible painter, period.

Please understand: I'm not against comfort and cozy. I am against *only* comfort and cozy, though. I want *both* the comfort and the conviction of God represented equally here: highlighters and colored pencils, sweat and blood sharing space on the pages of my Bible. I want to meet Him wrapped inside the warm blanket on my fluffy armchair *and* on my knees bruised by prayer. I want my eyes to light up with encouragement *and* my brow wrinkled from a furrowed contemplation of His holiness. Personally, I want scribbles more than I want calligraphy—scratched out all over my soul and the margins of His Word.

He meets me in the beauty and in the mess, and I'm tired of cleaning up my life for some invisible photograph before I come to Him. I can't do this anymore because it's costing me something really important—the fullness of Jesus, the one that meets me in both the beautiful ambiance of essential oil hippie life and on the kitchen counter surrounded by stale Cheerios, calling me to His invitation to make order out of my chaos.

The problem is not with the c's; I hope you understand that. The problem is I am acting like God is limited in where and when He will meet me, and that's just not true.

He is so, so much more than an Instagram-worthy God, and we are missing out when we reduce Him to such.

I want to meet with the Jesus who bled and died and cried; the one who went to the bathroom and was so human that people heard, felt, saw, and knew Him. The Jesus who probably didn't own a leather-bound version of the Torah but knew God honored a contrite and willing heart, no matter how it was packaged. The Jesus who decided to be born to a lowly peasant girl, in a smelly cattle stall, to bring true comfort to a messy, broken people.

He wants to meet with us—all the versions of us—and call our mess into life.

And here I am, accepting His gracious invitation.

SIXTEEN

choosing a characteristic

Choosing a major can feel like the biggest commitment and the scariest thing you've ever done in your life. Take it from me—I might have only changed majors once, but I seriously considered switching again approximately eleven different times over my sophomore year. I cried in bathroom stalls and researched occupations and graduate programs endlessly, desperate for some direction.

More on that later. For now, I want to share with you one really cool epiphany I had about choosing majors and careers during that difficult time, and it is this: *each career reflects an aspect of God.*

Just think about it—in our life's work, we are all acting out a finite characteristic of an infinite God. It's kind of like you get to choose which characteristic of God you want to pursue professionally.

Artists, inventors, and entrepreneurs *create* and *adorn*.

Doctors, nurses, and medical professionals physically *heal*.

Counselors and psychologists mentally and emotionally *heal*.

Stay-at-home mothers *nurture* and *discipline*.

Stockbrokers and bankers are *stewards* and *advisors*.

Governing positions *govern*.

Architects and construction workers *build* and *mold*.

contemplations of a collegiate christian

Pastors play the role of *shepherd*.

Teachers and professors *teach* their students.

Accountants *restore* chaotic finances.

Fashion designers and boutique owners *clothe* us with beauty.

Lawyers, judges, and police officers *enforce justice*.

Farmers, chefs, and restaurant workers *sustain* our hunger and *nourish* our bodies.

Plumbers provide water to wash us, to *quench* our thirst.

Garbage men remove and help us *dispose of—trim away*—what is unhelpful in our lives.

Store owners *provide* for our material needs.

Whatever you choose to do with the talents God has given you, if you do it in a godly way, you are mirroring part of His character. What an honor!

We really are made in His image, in every facet, even professionally. So much so, that every single moment of our days—even our professional lives—can reflect who He is, if we so choose to embrace our roles.

Therefore, when you choose a major, even though it can be a big commitment and a daunting affair, it can also be a very exciting moment! What aspects of God will you reflect in your career?

Though there is much wisdom in taking into account one's salary, benefits, holiday time, and other logistics, I hope you do consider two other facets deeply as well. I wish I had given these things their due respect; these two considerations have aided greatly in my single-minded commitment to the career calling God has on my life.

The first consideration is what aspect of God you have a natural ability for. What skills has He gifted you with?

choosing a characteristic

This is more than the "follow your heart" message many generations have received. Many of us have heard our passions are not mistakes, so we should follow our passions! And sure, there's definitely truth to that. However, I would also add that our skills are not mistakes either. If God blueprinted your soul, body, and mind to be exceptional at something, then that thing is worth exploring. It's worth investing in, too—possibly, in your career life.

For a long time, I didn't use my writing skills very much in my professional life. I have always been gifted with words, but I considered this skill to only be my hobby. Even though biology and anatomy weren't really my fortes, I was too busy pursuing a career in the medical field to give a second thought to writing professionally. Eventually, I realized God gave me this gift of writing, and I should really take time to maximize it, instead of forcing myself into a mold He didn't design me for.

If you aren't sure what your skills are, take time to consider this. These are the abilities your parents and friends have pointed out in you, something you are particularly talented at, which separates you from the average person. It's the thing you naturally just thrive at, for some reason, and you don't really know why. Not that you're already a pro at it, but you just don't struggle as much as the average person. Consider that thing and professions that involve those skills. You might not be dying to pursue one of them, but give it a chance. Maybe research it a little. Play around with the idea, and go shadow someone in that field. You just might be surprised how God uses your talent both for your delight and His glory.

The second consideration is this: what aspect of God is mirrored in this profession?

Like I pointed out earlier, each career has an aspect of God's character. When we can pinpoint this characteristic and focus on it during our workdays, it makes our professions much more thrilling.

Ponder this: in your (potential) profession, you will bear God's character, God's image, God's love to the world through your career. Think of all the specifics for your job.

As a writer and author, I am a steward of thoughts and ideas. The Bible verses about the weightiness of words and the power of the tongue become even more real to me in my profession. My words are a big deal, not because I'm an awesome author but because words matter to God. I am serving as a representative of the God on high, the holiest One, and my written words are a part of the representation. Pondering this makes typing away on a Tuesday morning much more invigorating; I'm stewarding a thing of great value; I'm working as a representative of the Most High.

Image-bearing, gospel-centered professions aren't restricted to those in ministry. The entirety of our days, every hour, every moment can be ministry. You can preach the Gospel through grace-filled words, through a commitment to integrity in your college courses, through intentional kindness at the grocery store, through service to your family, and you can most definitely preach the Gospel through your 8-to-5 job, in a million ways. Be it integrity, hard work, kindness, responsibility, grace-filled words, faithfulness, refusal to gossip or put down your co-workers—this is all gospel work.

College is preparing you for excellence in your field of interest, and if you ask Him, God will equip you for image-bearing in that field. You will spend a huge amount of time in your career, and it is not wasted when it's lived for His glory. Your career will not go unnoticed or unseen; it is seen by the Maker of the universe.

Colossians 3:23-24 (ESV) encourages believers in this pursuit, making it clear that all of our work (*"whatever we do"*) is, ultimately, for the glory of God and not for men:

> *Whatever you do, work heartily, as for the Lord and not for men,*
> *knowing that from the Lord you will receive the inheritance*
> *as your reward. You are serving the Lord Christ.*

If you want to feel divine purpose and passion for your career, my advice as a rookie is to identify your skills, consider the God you are mirroring, and ponder that ultimately, you are working for Him. All of this will fuel your excellence, to the glory of God.

A career to the glory of God? That's a career worth working, a life worth living.

SEVENTEEN

a sacred addiction

"Grace comes into the soul, as the morning sun into the world; first a dawning; then a light; and at last the sun in his full and excellent brightness."

Thomas Adams

My roommates and I, like most college students, adored coffee.

Every morning, we consumed about two pots altogether, some of us drinking a little more than others, but all contributing our fair share. We were nothing but grateful to the person who braced the chill of morning, poured dark ground beans into their rightful place, and flicked the switch on the pot.

The sputter and kick of the pot, right before the trickle, is practically the sound of deliverance, a trumpet sound of revival.

Though we mostly preferred it dark, steaming, and as fresh as we could come by, we also didn't hold any prejudices—no coffee snobs resided there. (Okay maybe a few, but not enough of a snob to turn down a cup.) Bring it all, Folgers and fancy organic roasteries, extra dark Ethiopian roast, and light-roasted blueberry-cobbler flavored, and pour it in our cup. We would be grateful just the same.*

---

* It would have ruined the paragraph to say this, but we invited all except for Maxwell House. We would not be grateful for Maxwell. Please don't send it to us or we might have to vote to excommunicate you from our home. It tastes like burnt bean juice. Everything else is heavenly, roasty, toasty coffee, but Maxwell will be sure to plummet even the most heightened morning joy.

contemplations of a collegiate christian

I once wrote this little line that said "drink grace like coffee," and many people connected with it. Perhaps because far too many adults and college students have a bit of an addiction to the sweet golden-brown liquid, and all of us know we are in need of grace just the same.

The analogy seems to resonate still, this comparison between coffee and grace, and grace still serves as my sweet addiction. My relationship with coffee and with grace keeps me crawling back on hands-and-knees, desperate for more every single morning, all throughout daylight, and into the night, holding out my cup to the Lord, asking Him to fill it, make me holy, change me, renew me, let me taste Him.

So, here's to the coffee lovers, the sinners-turned-grace-addicts, who will understand this analogy like none other—this one is for us.

These three things are true of grace: it's nearly tangible, necessary, and offered freely, though it is costly. Coffee is tangible, nearly necessary, and a free gift in our home, since the price has been paid.

I have found, the more I taste the Gospel of Christ—that is, in short, that I was once a deeply flawed sinner, and yet, He loved so much that He died and rose again to save a rebellious human like me—grace becomes both bitter and sweet. It is rich and profound in its complexity, striking me down and building me up, disciplining me, making me rely on Christ more and more.

The complex paradox of grace is this: when we give Him rebellion, He gives us love. And all we can do is come to Him and hold out our empty, broken, leaking cups, once at salvation, and over and over again in our sanctification. All we do is receive, over and over and over, as He pours grace into us and changes us. He pours Himself out like a never-ending well, and we receive His grace like always-thirsty humans, allowing it to enter the bloodstream of our souls, changing us from the inside out, sealing our cracks, and mending our brokenness.

This is the healing, incomprehensible cycle of grace: it's humility that leads to freedom, admitting our brokenness that leads to wholeness, exposing our emptiness that leads to fullness. I offer my empty and shattered cup, and He uses it, re-forming all my broken pieces, filling me up, reviving me, energizing me to love Him with all I have.

a sacred addiction

That's why the Gospel makes zero and total sense at the same time. It seems like robbery, except that He has an endless supply of grace, and He's not mad about giving it away. It's actually His great joy; He's inviting us in for our fill.

Like making my morning cup of coffee, experiencing grace involves crawling out of my slumber, shuffling to the coffee pot, and holding out nothing but an empty mug, asking Him to fill me up, asking Him to meet me with a daily dosage of this bittersweetness.

And sure enough, His promised portion, rich and inviting, pours itself out, waking my heart up to the wonders and new mercies promised to believers with each ordinary twirl of the globe, each twenty-four hour period, and every minute along the way.

Sometimes grace is warm and inviting, sweet, kind, and comforting.

Sometimes grace burns your tongue a little, tasting a little bitter, making you scrunch your nose, leaving a trace of conviction down your esophagus and into your core. You know you *need* it, though, that conviction, that bitterness, in order to get the full experience.

No matter the day, grace wakes you up from your slumber and meets you with the reality of sinner-turned-saint, by faith alone, through His love alone.

Grace has become more vital, more real, more tactical in my morning routine. Grace, like coffee, has become almost tangible—like the feel of my canvas Bible cover, the flipping of the pages, a pencil between my teeth, eyes drooping but heart ready for His Word—these movements, this rhythm electrifies my soul, and it has become an essential ritual to living my best, most glorifying, most satisfying days.

Just like smelling the roasty, toasty, uncomfortable yet comforting first steaming sip of coffee, opening the pages of Scripture is promising, elemental, physical, warm, sometimes sharp and bitter with conviction, but in the end, always reviving. The Word allows my soul a sigh of relief: revival is cupped here in my hands.

I come groggy, tired, disillusioned, and low on hope. His Word comes fresh and new to stun my soul, convict my mind, warm my spirit, awaken my weary heart. I bask and simultaneously snuggle in the Gospel for a moment. It sobers me to the bitterness of deep sin and separation and awakens me to the contrasting love of a sacrificial Savior.

We bring hollow souls, and He fills, breaks, rebuilds, warms, and energizes our shells of humanity, so we can sing praises to Him and fill others' cups with the pour we've been given.

Grace allows us to praise our Father on high, the great grace provider, and to invite others to praise Him too so we can sing like David, "my cup overflows" (Psalm 23:4).

We reach into a hardened and frozen world, full of cold souls,

inviting them in for an hour of warmth,

enticing them with a cup of coffee,

inviting them in for an overflowing,

never-ceasing cup of Grace with the Savior of our souls.

EIGHTEEN

the mid-college crisis

"The labor of God is to trust in the Son"
Jenny and Tyler, *"Abide"*

There came a time during my junior year where a mid-college crisis sneakily struck my soul.

Its origin was a small thought—nothing too disastrous to my peace of mind. It began with, "Maybe I will apply to graduate school." That turned into, "Wow, writing is a really cool thing that I'm decently gifted at, but has nothing to do with any of my past experience." From there it became, "Oh, I just realized that in a year from now, I need to have an idea of what I might want to do for the rest of my earthly days. I need to know how I will provide for myself and possibly a future family, what health insurance means, how to both comprehend and complete things like federal taxes, and how to sell my measly resume composed of babysitting and a couple of unrelated side jobs to a real-life company that probably won't give a fadoozle that I was on the honor roll."

All pleasant thoughts.

Initially, the thoughts seemed harmless. I was a science major who was falling hard for writing. Maybe these two paths could be combined, I thought. This consideration was harmless, until it turned into, "What if I mess it all up?" and "What if I ruin my life by choosing the wrong major?" and "Did I already screw it all up? Is it too late? Am I destined for a failed and unsatisfying career?" All of which made me weep uncontrollably almost every day like a madwoman and had me obsessively researching which career was best for "my personality type." I tumbled into an identity crisis, visiting seven different professors within one month, asking each of them to diagnose my heart's condition, leaving me feeling hopeless when they only advised me in choosing next semester's courses instead of my entire life's course.*

What began as small anxieties in the crevices of my heart, grew roots there, and wreaked havoc on my entire self—mind, body, and spirit. Anxiety for my post-college life called the shots in both my cognition and emotion.

Anxiousness results from losing our perceived control. It's a result of being "divided" as the Greek word would literally translate. Divided between godly affection and worldly affection. Divided between worldly concerns and godly concerns. Split.

And divided temples… don't stand. They crumble, actually. They weep and wail. They don't have solid ground.

Since I continued in my division of soul, neglecting to eradicate my small anxieties with Truth, they grew into large anxieties. I remained ungrounded in the greater reality of my human adulting: that a loving God knew every detail and He was Lord of it. If I simply sought His face, He would take care of the rest (Matthew 6:33, Isaiah 26:3).

Instead, I was too busy trying to be my own god, trying to trust my own instinct, trying to establish my own plan. I failed to remember I am a creature, and He is the Creator. I am a servant, and He is the king. The order was out of whack, and so my temple was a wreck.

All I had to do was trust He was guiding me, submit to His truth of provision, even if it felt completely unlike anything I would have chosen. All I had to do was believe His Spirit was guiding me. But I was afraid.

So afraid.

Instead of praying and remembering God's proven goodness, reminding myself He had kept me well-fed and sheltered for twenty years and could continue to do so, instead of reading verses about His care for children like me, submitting

---

* *When they didn't play the role of Jesus for me, I panicked. Imagine that.*

myself to my sheep-ness, and asking Him to be my shepherd, I tried to advise, research, and rationalize myself out of my fears.

Rationalizing oneself out of fear isn't a great tactic. You just might find, as I did in my case, that instead of comfort, all you can see are the endless ways you could ruin everything. It ended in a manic version of myself, googling "jobs for my personality type" or "what even is my personality type" or "what to do when you have a mid-college crisis" or "how not to end up homeless." Then I dialed a panic call to my best friend, my mom, my boyfriend, the professor I felt would be my best friend if we were born in the same decade, and my newly-appointed counselor.

Once, I'm ashamed to admit, I spent $25 of my measly college budget to take a "special, new, intensive personality assessment that will help you figure out your dream job!" This did nothing beyond telling me I shouldn't have gone to college in the first place. (Yay.) I spent hours pouring my heart out to my friends about my fears of post-graduation. I stayed up at night frantically researching the "perfect career" for "flighty" Enneagram sevens and "wishful" ENFPs.

I was petrified of everything that could go wrong, of the ways that adulthood was painful and hard, of my own inadequacies, of parting ways with my best friends and roommates, of the terrifying idea of choosing to spend the rest of my life with someone, even though I dearly loved him.

I let all of my fears define my future self, and so I began to fear her—my future me—most of all. I imagined myself out of college, a mediocre 9-to-5 job that was so terribly boring and lifeless, with no friends or family nearby, alone and unknown, not being connected with the Church in intimate and convicting ways, eating Thai take-out every night, and trying to fit into a pantsuit the next day.

I did this for months. It wreaked havoc on my mind, my relationships, and my intimacy with God. I could not see clearly, and my hope was running dry because I was trying to predict the future, was preparing for things I had not yet been assigned, and set my hope in my idea of a "perfect life" I thought I could somehow obtain with my weak strivings.

The mid-college crisis can be very real.

contemplations of a collegiate christian

But what I found is, though it is very real, it isn't true.

Yes, if you are thinking about changing your major or career path, it's probably going to be scary. You might wonder if you will be able to hold a steady job and afford to eat. You will question if all the time you spent in your past classes was a waste. You might even have to add an extra semester, or even year, of college onto your five-year plan. You might not be sure where you're headed or what the end goal is.

But no, you aren't crazy or a lunatic or irresponsible simply because you feel God calling you into something different from what you previously thought. No, you aren't ridiculous because you started listening more closely to His heart for your life than the world. No, you don't need to explain your mid-college crisis to every stranger you meet. Actually, it doesn't even have to be a crisis—it can simply be a change. A change you are submitting to and trusting to the Lord.

That's the Christian life. Our plans change when God gives us directions that don't match up with our five-year, ten-year, or life plan, and we choose to trust Him because He has proven Himself trustworthy.

I hope you can believe that. Careers and life plans change sometimes, and that's okay. God knew this would happen, and He isn't letting go of you. I wish I would have spent more time believing that and less time believing I had to have it all figured out.

Having walked through that season now, I'm trying to focus more on His heart, His character, His provision rather than my own. So, next time I have a crisis, I'm going to stop trying to find the answers and just do the labor He calls me to in the moment: to do what is set before me today and to trust Him with the rest.

Trust is much better than control—it allows us to take bread for the day, for the present hour and not hoard it for the years ahead. It gives me a breather, where I can let go of all the control I cling so tightly to, and to set my hope, not in a comfortable life, but in the One who has provided abundant life all along.

I was looking for any bit of control, but God asked for my trust. He was inviting me to trust in new mercies for a new season.

the mid-college crisis

I remember a day when my mind, soul, and body were worn from a year of fighting. I had been fighting God's providence, trying to take the reins, to people-please and self-satisfy. I remember when I stopped trying to control every single aspect of the post-college season, and simply prayed, asking God to provide me with the daily things I needed for the years ahead. I asked Him to help me let go of control.

I had never felt such peace.

Anxiety is common in college, and it's become really, really common in our generation. Millennials are diagnosed with severe anxiety twice as much as baby boomers were, and sixty-three percent of college students experience frequent anxiety. This is only one small statistic, but just search "anxiety and millennials" or "Generation Z," and you will quickly realize no one is alone in this problem.

There's no doubt the core of this is our sinful nature, hormonal imbalances, or a mix of both. However, we must acknowledge that an increase in perceived control is likely aiding our disease. We are the generation that has been told we "can do anything we want to" and have been given devices that give us the illusion of ultimate knowledge and ultimate control. The illusion is so enticing, yet, it's just that: an illusion.

Ultimate knowledge and control were not anymore meant for us than it was meant for Adam and Eve. Don't allow chronological snobbery* to fog your thoughts; we are no better than the ancients. We are just as human. And in the same way that their desire for control was what cursed the rest of humanity, our striving for control will curse our lives if we cling to it.

When I realized I never had all the answers and I never will, I found His ways are sweeter, more satisfying than anything my finite mind can think up. I found He is a timeless, sovereign God, and we are present, finite creatures, just lucky enough to be loved by Him.

Prayer is hard when you're anxious because it seems to do so little. Speak

---

* An argument that the thinking, art, or science of an earlier time is inherently inferior to that of the present, simply by virtue of its temporal priority or the belief that since civilization has advanced in certain areas, people of earlier periods were less intelligent.

words to God? What will that change? I have found it might not change the situation, but it will change the most important piece of the puzzle: your heart.

Senior year, I committed to spending just as much time praying about my anxieties as I did researching graduate schools and possible jobs. I learned to breathe in and out, giving Him all of my "what-if's." I did my part within my design, and then I asked Him to carry my future in His hands.

Now, when I think about the future and feel my chest close a little tighter, the air becoming a little thinner, my forehead getting a little more wrinkled, I choose to remember what He brought me through in the past. I choose to remember I was never meant to hold the future. I choose to submit to my role in the present. I choose to remember the God who holds all of humanity's past, present, and future.

I remember the One who brought me to this university, where I thought I didn't want to go, and caused my cup to overflow.

I remember the One who gave me dignity when I was covered in nothing but hopelessness and shame during my freshman year.

I remember the One who brought me to my best friends, my sisters-in-Christ.

The One who was crushed so that I wouldn't have to be.

The One who sits at His right hand, proclaiming righteousness on our behalf at every millisecond of every day.

The One who effortlessly holds the entire Milky Way on the tip of His pinky, who sits enthroned above it all (Isaiah 40:22).

The One to whom I can cry, with all the angst in my soul, *"Abba, Daddy."*

The One who promises to never leave us, who guarantees to walk with us through every peak and valley of His will for our lives (Matthew 28:20).

He knows things we cannot yet know. We cannot rationalize or Google His will. But He really is worthy of our trust, and we can give Him our tears, our worries, our fears, and our mid-college crisis.

NINETEEN

the humility of learning

*"Time always flies, the hour (or two or three) leaving you
exhausted, happy, perturbed, and yet strangely satisfied by the
end. I was always grateful for the walk or bicycle ride back to
college, dinner, or the pub afterward to allow things to settle
or rise in my thoughts. The physical movement required to
navigate winding paths home aided the mental digestion... One's
degree at Oxford becomes for most not a matter of a prerequisite
for a job, or to please one's parents, or to make a minimum income
bracket. Rather, the opportunity to study here seals an experience
marked by intense personal growth resulting from a genuine desire
to learn. A heady, hearty experience that changes you forever
because it cracks you open ultimately to the humility of learning,
which is where all of this wanted to take you in the first place."*

Carolyn Weber, *Surprised by Oxford*

I love this quote because this is what college felt like for me: humiliating, but
the type of humiliation that doesn't just leave you there. It calls you to more,
resurrecting you from your previous ignorance, your own skewed view of the
world, your old habits of sin, ultimately from yourself altogether, and calls you
to higher, greater, and better knowledge.

Some people may associate higher education with arrogance, but I think if you
really learn something in college, you learn humility is the main lesson one
should take away from a university degree.

There is little rest for the weary at university. Big words on lessons on books
on interviews on statistics on new words on deep talks with friends on Bible

studies on seminars on podcasts on articles on newer words on more books all pile into my brain until I go into overdrive, and all of the sudden, I cannot remember the difference between "specific" and "Pacific," and I just need a long walk, a fresh cup of coffee, a temple massage, and a four-hour nap to digest all the knowledge consumed.

Then, of course, onto formulating a thesis for the next essay.

Higher education rightfully results in a higher level of thinking. It calls its students to exponential growth and change-mentally, emotionally, and for those of us who follow Jesus, spiritually as well. Nothing on campus is ever static, and consequently, no sense of permanence resides there. Once you've learned one thing, it's time to move on to the next. There are mountains to examine, and valleys to comprehend, each one shaping your mind in a new way, changing your view of the world, (hopefully) shifting you out of yourself. It became a common pattern for me to look up and fail to recognize the person I was even the month before, accounting for all the sprouting and blooming.

I realize that for many students, traditional education has been an unwelcome difficulty, boring at best and shameful at worst. For that, I am genuinely grieved. However, I bet there was one professor or one teacher that made you love the subject because they made it relevant to your life. They showed you why it mattered in your day-to-day interactions, and how the concepts you wrote about on your tests actually affected your reality.

Since discovering this bridge between the classroom and the world beyond campus, I have had a hard time separating my personal life from my academic life; I find myself searching for God's design in every physics lesson and in every page of literature, and His fingerprints are always so clear. The connection of academia and faith, whether it's in science, English, psychology, history, and or any discipline, is incredible and undeniable. Each discipline testifies to its Creator, and the puzzle of His fingerprints is glorious to slowly piece together.

Classes were often hard to swallow, like the giant pills I cried over when I was young. My mom made me take them anyway because it was "for my good." The discipline of studying was often overwhelming, surprising, and excruciating, but it was a good type of strain. I consider it a great opportunity to grapple so hard, to wrinkle my forehead so deeply, to consider things so intensely. It's an honor, this humility of learning and my academic disciplines have proven worthy of my time and effort.

My spiritual life paralleled this academic experience during that time, and it still does today. I am often lost in the middle of a spiritual lesson, confused and wondering how in the world I will wrap my mind around what God is teaching me in the moment. Sometimes, I'm not even sure what subject I am supposed to be absorbing. There are times when every answer to every question seems dark and mysterious, and I cannot figure out why I'm here or even where "here" is. There are days when, after praying and consulting Scripture and journaling and rationalizing and discussing, the problem of my heart is still not solved, and I must get up tomorrow and wrestle again, trusting that the rest will eventually come because my God promised it. And eventually, in due time, a spiritual sabbatical or epiphany finds its way into my soul.

There are those lessons I am still learning but I cannot yet speak into language because their confusion is too real. I know they have meaning, but God hasn't given me the words yet. But I obediently sit in the confusion, knowing clarity awaits (1 Corinthians 14:33).

The surest and looming question that kept me up at night, the lesson that college student dares to think and cry and wonder about:

Where is all of this leading me? Where will I go with this knowledge that feels so impractical at times? What does this mean after graduation? Why does this all matter anyway?

I have learned that this is the best type of learning, and the best lessons are those that you, in the middle of it all, cannot even figure out what is the overarching subject. It makes you trust Him, and hold on to Him tighter than the answers because you won't arrive at them until …well, He allows you to arrive.

Those are the sweetest lessons; those you did not even realize you needed to learn, those you couldn't have learned without walking through them, with Him. Those lessons take the longest, yet prove themselves most eternal and most noble.

I have learned to write through wrestling, to embrace the struggle, and to settle here in this messy scholarship of Grace.
I have learned to stop trying to flip to the end of the book, and instead, to read

this chapter, this page, this sentence only. To savor what He's allowed for this point in time. Time has taught me it is linear for a reason, that I must learn this lesson to fully appreciate and live the next one.

Through university life, God has taught me how to learn patiently:

by soaking in and treasuring wisdom necessary for the moment,

by hugging and embracing this present piece of the larger story,

and by feeling the cold confusion and the warm epiphanies equally.

Only in this does learning reach its highest form.

As one poet once said, it is vital to "live" all the questions.

> *"Be patient toward all that is unsolved in your heart and try to love the questions themselves, like locked rooms and like books that are now written in a very foreign tongue. Do not now seek the answers, which cannot be given you because you would not be able to live them. And the point is, to live everything."*
>
> Rainer Maria Rilke, *Letters to a Young Poet*

I definitely think we should seek the answers (Matthew 7:7), but I love the encouragement of patience towards the unsolved pieces of our minds and souls. They cannot all be understood in one day; if they could be, we wouldn't have to return to our Bibles or flip back to pages of old books or recite old heart-lessons, over and over again. Repetition is part of the process, and it must be given due honor.

These, after all, are the hardest lessons: those which make you come back for more. They are also the most important and exhilarating. I have concluded we are meant for a life of learning, and relearning, and relearning. I'm learning to live for this life of never-ending growth and regrowth. Though it might feel cyclical, I can feel my roots digging deeper into faith and reason in each turn.*

Being a student is one of the most cherished titles I have ever held. I love my university, my classes, my classmates, and my teachers. I want to gather all the notebooks, the anthologies, the academic arguments, and the logical epiphanies, and hold them close, breathe them in, let their depth seep into my very blood and transform me. I want to snuggle all of the lessons, so much so that I have an entire drawer full of American literature, physics, calculus, language, and cognitive psychology notes that I will request to be buried with me in my grave because I never want to go a day without learning something new about this world that He made, about the people He formed, about who He is and was and always will be.

I have also learned that I will always be a student—a student of the most high, most holy, most knowledgeable Christ. A student of the One who created knowledge itself. A student of the One from whom every lesson originates, and who teaches the most wonderful, eternal lessons of all.

He does not promise exquisite excerpts from eighteenth-century poets or contemplations on paradigm shifts or research methods that quantify the otherwise subjective. His lessons don't result in grades or degrees. Degrees and earthly knowledge are worthy of temporary admiration, but they are fading. What He promises is infinitely more valuable and eternal.

He promises to teach me the very most important things:

how to love the unlovable,

how to quiet a restless heart,

how to get on my knees and experience His presence,

the certainty and reason for faith in Him,

the magic of losing my life and in turn, gaining it,

the silent secret of sacrifice,

how to be the most content at rock-bottom,

---

* Faith and reason are not at odds. If you are tempted to think so, consider this quote form C.S. Lewis: "Faith, in the sense in which I am here using the word, is the art of holding on to things your reason has once accepted, in spite of your changing moods"

contemplations of a collegiate christian

the humility of learning as a disciple of Christ,

and the most mysterious, humbling lesson

of an ancient, broken, Jewish God-man

who dared die for

silly,
trembling,
stumbling

       students like me.

TWENTY

the secret place

"Would you like to know sweetness the secret of the Lord?
Go and hide beneath His shadow; this shall then be your reward;
And whene'er you leave the silence of that happy meeting place,
You must mind and bear the image of His face"

But Jesus often withdrew to the wilderness for prayer.
Luke 5:16, NLT

College will break you, crush you, have you on your knees at some point. There's no escaping it; it can be a merciless experience.

This moment might come to you late at night in the library or during a winter break. It will probably come multiple times, in waves, washing all sanity away. It will likely cause you to Google something to the effect of "how much money do plumbers make?" (It's actually a decent living— go for it!) You might find yourself near despair on a regular basis, wondering if you could just un-enroll and try something else.

There will be times when you cry on your way to class, when you hope your roommate doesn't hear your sniffles, when you just wish you could get a solid eight hours of rest.

I speak from experience: this is the exact moment to hone in on your best weapon: the life-giving, heart-renewing power of prayer.

The ramblings of these pages, these after and middle-of-the-moment thoughts are brought to you, sweet readers, by none other than prayer itself.

Tell Him what is on your heart, truly. Follow C.S. Lewis' advice to "lay before him what is in us; not what ought to be in us." If that means head-in-hands, knees-aching, "don't You hear me?" the "where are You?", lost-for-words kind of prayer, so be it. David prayed like that at times. Maybe it's the kind that wears you out, like sobbing over a movie about cancer and death. The kind that's laborious and lamenting. The kind that makes you forget you're in public or that you have a body. The kind of prayer you surrender to. Urgent and intense, acknowledging the reality of, "I'm not okay at all God, but I know that You can answer me and lift me out of this if You so choose." The acknowledgment to your Father that something is just not right, and you need to hear from Him.

Some people avoid prayer because it requires time and effort. Some people don't believe it will change anything. Some people don't pray because they are too busy rehearsing the circumstances over and over, ranting to anyone with ears, trying to rationalize themselves out of the pain and hurt and fear that feels so freakishly close.* Others simply forget about it.

Many of us, I believe, are afraid of this kind of prayer because it requires genuine vulnerability. It feels scary to get lost in prayer, to admit something hurts so badly. Maybe if I ignore my pain and frustration, it will go away, we rationalize. Maybe if I can just recite a Bible verse, it will serve as a band-aid on my aching wound.

Please don't fall into these traps. Prayer isn't for the holier-than-thou. It's for the sinners-turned-saints. It's for the desperate. It's for the sick. It's for the needy. It's for creatures like us. It's for *humans*.

Prayer is a *gift* to us; it's meant for our good. It shouldn't be a burden or a to-do list. It's an honor to set before the throne of God your hurts and desires and ask Him to edify you and set you straight.

So get down on your dusty dorm room floor. Go into the bathroom stall. Stop

---

Admittedly, I often fall into this last category. Tip for those of us who do: rationalizing your situation won't make it any less painful. Take it to God.

in the campus chapel. Get in your car and drive. Head out to the middle of the woods if you have to. (Jesus did.) Do anything you can to get there, to meet with Him, to retreat and cry *out*.

Tell Him the deep stuff, the things you spend the most thought on, the things you hold so tightly to, the things that are dimming your spirit. Tell Him why social media haunts you, and you're ashamed of your body and your grades and you never feel good enough. Tell Him why you're hurting. Tell Him the sin that clings so closely. Tell Him that you don't know why you're hurting. Tell Him the frustrations in your family and your bleeding friendships. Tell Him how you can't muster up much faith anymore to see Him in His word.

And after all of the hurt, after you've processed it together, after you've cried all the tears, *ask*.

Ask Him to enter it all, to fill in all the gaps. To heal every wound and confusion and scar. To untangle your confusion. To let go of what you can't control. To change your perspective. To give you the eyes to see Him, the ears to hear Him, to trust Him again. Tell Him your faith is running low, and you need revival, and you can't do this without Him.

He promises to meet us here, in this heart posture of humility. Here in this place, you invite Him in to fill all your gaps and mend all your cracks. It might take time. It might take a lot of knocking, but persistence is part of the journey (Luke 11:5-13, 18:1-7), and prayer is anything but a waste of time. Prayer includes resigning control, but it isn't passive. It's actively admitting your weakness and putting on Christ's strength. It's the step in moving forward from fear into faith, from hurting into healing, from trials into triumph.

The only way to heal is through vulnerability, this deep humility of admitting you can't do it alone.

Allow Him to expose your weaknesses, and then let Him coddle you like one would comfort a squirming baby that just feels sad, lonely, afraid, tired, and desperate for something and doesn't know what (Romans 8:26-27).

Don't turn to the internet. It doesn't care whether you are grounded in truth; it just wants the next click, the next anxious plea typed into a search bar. Don't even turn to friends or family first; they are human and the only knowledge they can possess is from Him anyway. Search for wisdom in the counsel of the godly, but don't look for the answers anywhere else but in God. And definitely—for goodness' sake—don't turn to yourself.

The internet isn't looking out for your best, college student.

Humans are flawed, dear one.

You are powerless in your own strength.

Open up the Word. Ask Him to speak. Call on the One who cares, who is looking out, who knows more than you, who will shift your eyes back to His face, your ears back to His voice, your heart back to His own.

Pray.

TWENTY ONE

finity amidst abundance

"We are finite beings trying to live an infinite life."
A quote from my journal in April 2019, my junior year of college

This realization cut me to the core. I felt so exposed by my own mind because I knew this was it exactly. This was my problem. If my name were in the dictionary the definition would be "Mary Madeline: n. a finite being trying to live an infinite life."*

I think we are all a bit this way, but in college, this condition of mine really bubbled to the surface. I am an experience junkie. Be it food, travel, dancing, socializing, interesting courses, seminars, whatever—I want to eat it, drink it, do it, take it, learn it, know it, to be part of it, to experience it. I want to soak in every experience, just for the sake of the thrill, as much as I possibly can. My heart often screams the anthem of *carpe diem*!

Though I feel like the queen of this sickness, it seems that younger generations are experiencing this more than ever in what Jill Carattini, calls "a cultural eco-system where we worship possibilities":

> *"There is a phrase in Latin that summarizes the idea that the shape of our deepest affections is the shape of our lives.* Lex orandi, lex credendi, lex vivendi *is the axiom of ancient Christianity, meaning: the rule of worship is the rule of belief is the rule of life. That is, our deepest*

---

* By "finite" I do not mean in our experience of our experience after death, since we will all exist on into eternity. By finite, I simply mean "limited." Humans have limits God does not have. For a good book on this, I suggest Jen Wilkin's None Like Him.

contemplations of a collegiate christian

*affections (whatever it might be that we focused on most devotedly)
shapes the way we believe and, in turn, the way we live. In a cultural
ecosystem where we seem to worship possibilities, where freedom is
understood as the absence of limitation upon our choices, and where
the virtue of good multitasking has replaced the virtue of singleness
of heart, it is understandable that we are both truly and metaphorically
'all over the place'— mentally, spiritually, even bodily, in a
state of perpetual possibility-seeking."*

I know what it is like to be all over the place in every way possible. This was me during college. I wanted it *all* within those four years: all the fun and all of the achievement, all the travel and all the money-saving, all of the freedom of singles and all the intimacy of a relationship, all of the study abroad programs and all experience of living an American college life, all of the wit of an English major and all the prestige of an engineering major, all of the classes and all of the free time. I couldn't even commit to an entire summer doing one thing; usually, I would make a one-month commitment so I could switch plans in the middle of the summer, not missing out on family time, travel, or a cool internship. Singleness of heart was far from me.

I wanted to squeeze every last drop of juice out of every single fruit I could in college. The only problem was this: the possibilities were endless, and yet, as a limited creature, I possessed an end.

I wanted those four years to be infinite, but more than that, *I* wanted to be infinite—not in the eternal sense, but in the without-limitations sense.

Striving to experience it all was suffocating, because humans weren't made for this. We were made for an eternity of course, but we weren't made for infinity. When we try to be infinite, we become divided.*

I was deceived into the lie that an abundance of "freedom" (i.e.: endless choices of opportunities and possibilities) would be my joy. Yet, I found they could never fulfill. It took me most of college, but I eventually learned I will not experience all that my flesh wants to experience. It's unobtainable, and it isn't what we were made for.

---

* Remember? We just discussed being divided in spirit a few pages ago.

finity amidst abundance

But there's a greater treasure, and this treasure *is* obtainable: submitting to my limited nature, and striving for singleness of heart rather than a divided one. I find extreme contentment and joy when I submit my spirit to its finiteness, when I use all of my energy to enjoy God within the realm of possibility I have been given. I will experience what my heart has been searching for all along when I recognize I am limited, and I am to function within my limits.

Since we are limited, and we cannot "have it all," that means we have to *choose* in college. Personally, I had to choose between majors, relationships, commitments, and all the things I wanted to fill up on. Often, I found myself at crossroads, and the choices paralyzed me down deep in my soul, causing deep anxiety. What do you mean I don't get it all? How am I supposed to be content with my finite nature? Choices seemed to threaten my freedom, but what I later learned was that they actually aided in my freedom. That is the freedom of single-mindedness.

The Apostle Paul's words rang in my head:

> *...for I have learned in whatever situation I am to be content. I know how to be brought low, and I know how to abound. In any and every circumstance, I have learned the secret of facing plenty and hunger, abundance and need. I can do all things through him who strengthens me.*
> Phillippians 4:11b-13, ESV

I always thought it was funny that Paul talked about the ability to be content within abundance. I mean, who can't be content in abundance, Paul? Isn't that the easiest place to be content?

My college experience attested to a resounding "no." I had an abundance of everything to choose from: careers, friends, opportunities, events, clubs, and so on. Yet, my abundance just aggravated my desire to control and be filled with earthly things. The fun experiences only made me hunger for more excitement, the knowledge only proved to be one bite of a giant cake, and one coffee date made me just want ten more. I couldn't find true satisfaction in the state of abundance.

Maybe that's what the author meant when he wrote,
> *...give me neither poverty nor riches; feed me with the food that is needful for me, lest I be full and deny you and say, "Who is the LORD?"*

contemplations of a collegiate christian

or lest I be poor and steal and profane the name of my God.
Proverbs 30:8b-9, ESV

I think the author understood his sinful nature so well. He knew that within scarcity, he would mistrust God. Within abundance, he would try to have it all and be distracted from his truest need, God Himself.

I began to pray the same prayer during college, a prayer for singleness of heart:

Give me only what I need to worship and enjoy you well— nothing more, nothing less.

Through this journey of submission to my finiteness, I found joy. I found that getting the most out of college isn't doing everything possible in four years, squeezing all the experiences into such a slim time frame, making yourself exhausted on busyness or high on excitement 24/7. Instead, getting the most out of college is kinder, more simple, and more attainable than that. It looks like letting go of the millions of possibilities for your day in order to submit to the Holy Spirit's leading. It looks like saying "no" to some events and options so that time can be filled with prayer and the Word.

We get one college era, one life. Like our Savior said, so what if I gain the whole world, but lose my soul? What does it matter if I am high on life and experiences in college, but lose my intimacy with God in the process? What's the gain? There is none. It's nothing but an absolute, certain loss.

Choosing to overload oneself is enticing, no doubt. But I don't want to lose time with the Lord to a few fleeting, empty years of college high. I don't want to trade in intimacy with the Holy Spirit for a few fun dates, parties, or cool clubs I could join.

As I allowed God to slowly unpry my hand from the college rush, from the never-ending possibilities, letting go of the longing to be more, do more, see more, hear more of the things going on on campus, I learned to channel that energy into seeking Him, hearing from Him, doing for Him, being more of who He called me to be.

What an eternal investment for such a finite being like myself.

finity amidst abundance

Instead of trying to shove everything into four years or shove all of eternity into one life, I am learning to trust that my daily bread is enough. Like Paul, I am learning contentment in all situations—even in abundance.

It's a skill that must be practiced and gleaned but is worth it.

Because *He* is worth it.

He is worthy of our four years,

He is worthy of our lives.

TWENTY TWO

His four corners

"There is nothing like looking, if you want to find something. You certainly usually find something, if you look, but it is not always quite the something you were after."

J.R.R. Tolkien

In my twenty-two years on Earth, I have had the opportunity to visit about twenty-five states, eight countries, and four continents. In my college years, I flew across the globe completely alone and twice took summer internships in cities where I did not know a soul.

Though the prospect of foreign places is daunting at times, printing a plane ticket, planning stops, reserving an AirB&B, stuffing all my belongings into one backpack, and flipping through a passport always gives me a rush. Each action feels like endless potential—potential to learn, grow, see, taste, smell, breathe in the diversity of the world. Potential to learn His lessons and listen to the stories that come with physically being in a different place on the globe.

My travels look a lot different than Pinterest or a travel blogger's website. I definitely don't have the best pictures or "never-shift-from-this" advice. I can give some tips on how to save money, the best destinations at certain times of the year, which tourist traps to avoid, etcetera, but my philosophy on foreign adventure goes beyond advice on budgeting, booking the right ticket at the right time of year, or packing the perfect backpack.

Practical details and basic information are important, but the most important thing about traveling is simply learning to embrace the place, the people, and the experiences put right in front of you.

contemplations of a collegiate christian

Travel is so much less about taking control of your time, hitting every single hot-spot; so much less about calculating the best outcome for your budget (although I do recommend that), and so much more about letting the time, cities, roads, planes, and the people take you over; letting Him show you this world that He made—celebrating and aching equally.

The best trips are not those with five-star hotels, Instagram-worthy photographs, and window seats, though these things are not bad.

The best trip is the one where you get a great deal on the fancy hotel and laugh while you're using the restroom because *who knew about heated toilet seats*? The best trip is also the one where you pay practically nothing to giggle yourself to sleep in a sketchy hostel with forty other people in the same room, using your towel as a blanket because bedding wasn't included in the $29. It's both the hike where you get that totally unexpected photograph of that giant elk looking straight at you and the hike where your phone dies, so you have to remember the view from the top of the mountain through your memories and a detailed account in your journal. It's the day when you aimlessly wander through the city libraries and century-old cemeteries and the day when an expensive tour guide tells you every fascinating detail about every brick that built the city. It's a white cloth table set-for-two with wine, a sunset skyline, and pizza-by-the-slice in Central Park. It's striking up a four-hour-long conversation with the random Irish couple at the local pub, but also spending a solitary night with people watching through the streets of London. It's the holiday when you serve at a homeless shelter and hear men's stories about finding their place in their city but also when you have front-row tickets to a Broadway show.

The best part about cities, people, and places are that if you listen and follow, they will tell you their story. The old man with a newspaper and a five-o'clock shadow at the grungy diner will talk if you ask, and the local bus driver will tell you more details and local stories than a tour guide ever could. If your heart is soft enough, and you choose to be open, God will grow your love for this broken world beyond belief, city by city.

It's embracing the places and the people for the paradox that they are because our stories all have a little of the dazzling and dusty, the dirt and gold, the ugly and beautiful. The stories of people tell the story of a city. Each tattered soul that roams the streets is a piece of this magical, wonderful thing we call a community, people knit together by this literal common ground.

His four corners

The best road trips, international ventures, and next-town-over day trips are ones where we arrive with a grateful spirit, open our hearts to the complexity of community, and leave praising God for the opportunity to explore this diverse world that we will spend our lifetimes discovering; ones He called into being with a simple breath.

Whether you are a college student on summer break, new parents with a weekend without the kids, or seventy-five, retired and you want to go explore somewhere new, remember this: the outcome of the visit lies not in your ability to map the best route or find the best tour guide, but in your willingness to embrace your place, honor the paradox of humanity, and praise the One who made it all.

ripples in time and space

"My mind seems to have become a kind of machine for grinding general laws out of large collections of facts...if I had to live my life again, I would have made a rule to read some poetry and listen to some music at least once every week; for perhaps the parts of my brain now atrophied would thus have been kept active through use. The loss of these tastes is a loss of happiness, and may possibly be injurious to the intellect, and more probably to the moral character, by enfeebling the emotional part of our nature."

Charles Darwin

For the better part of my junior year, I considered pursuing a Ph.D in cognitive psychology.* I loved learning about the brain's cognitive functions, and I had an insatiable appetite for language research. These things still fascinate me to this day, and I love to look through old notes and remember the things I learned in my classes.

It seemed obvious I would head to graduate school to pursue a Ph.D., but I eventually decided against it the summer before my senior year. It was a hard decision, one that had me crying and praying for a month, but once the decision was final, I felt it was right in my soul.

I often operate under the assumption that the combination of skill and opportunity equates to a calling, but I'm not so sure this is always the case. Sometimes the paths that make the least sense are those the Lord is calling us down, and it

---

This is basically just the study of any sort of mental process in the brain, which includes a thousand things, such as reasoning, memory, attention, perception, etc. I was interested in studying human perception of language.

might seem crazy to the rest of the world, but as we rely on godly wisdom, not on the world's wisdom, peace guards us.

The reasons I decided to not pursue a Ph.D. were numerous, but the main one was this: I felt that I clung too closely to the knowledge I learned in the classroom, and I wanted to cling more closely to God instead of academia. In essence, cognitive psychology was becoming an idol for me, something that brought me more joy than time with God, something that I looked to for answers before looking to God. So, I felt diving head-first into a career of nothing but cognitive psychology was dangerous for me spiritually. More than being a professor or a researcher, I wanted to be Jesus' disciple. So, after months of prayer, wisdom-seeking, and fearful tears, the Lord gave me the strength to decide I would not pursue a Ph.D.

What started out as a tiny, intrusive, and scary thought of pursuing writing instead of psychology grew legs and started walking. For the girl who was always ten steps ahead of the game in the classroom, and as the first-born who was expected to be the responsible kid, it felt a bit weird and unsettling to admit that I wasn't going down a traditional path.

Telling others of my plans was an odd thing. I felt as if I was more so admitting to myself than admitting it to them. It felt like speaking the plan into existence. Announcing it felt like standing up, looking at my fears of inadequacy in the face, and balling my hand into a fist, ready to punch. I was shaking from fear of failure because I was so used to the easy, less-risky path, but I also had a deep peace that this was where God was leading me. I believed there was something beyond the fear that I couldn't see, simply because I was standing in the middle of the confusion.

The anxieties did linger in my soul for a season: *if I don't have my education or intelligence, who am I? If I don't pursue a doctorate, am I wasting my potential?*

I walked through my senior year, asking those same questions, but I felt the Lord leading me to writing, and I trusted Him. I became involved in the writing business, won some awards for my collegiate newspaper, graduated, and after COVID took a hit at the writing market, found a job as a nanny, and worked on publishing this book. I still don't know exactly where writing will lead, but I know I'm supposed to be here now, and that's what "walking in faith" is:

following the Lord's leading, one step at a time, even when we don't know the next step.

I know that for some, choosing a Ph.D. would have been the hard choice, but for me, it would have been the easy one. I am an excited learner, a hard thinker, and a big-time nerd. Graduate school seemed like the natural and safest progression. Considering anything else seemed irrational. To me, a writing career seems scary and a little too unpredictable, too unstable, too unregulated, out of my control. It takes a lot of faith for me to be here. The best part, though, is how it also feels a little too exciting—like I could not be invited into a career quite this thrilling, like I misread the invitation.

Though I'm dedicated to my career choice now, there were times where I just wanted the security of someone's approval so badly when I told them about my post-college plans, that I thought of resorting back to the safe plan. I would deceptively interrogate myself, *"Why not just go for the Ph.D., Mary Mad? Who could it hurt?"*

The obvious answer? Myself. Had I pursued the degree, it would only have been to prove my worth and intelligence and to avoid the disapproval of others. I had tried proving my worth before; it didn't lead anywhere worthwhile. I decided I had to stop doing things to prove myself to others, and I must start working towards the things that I most believed in.

So whenever I was ready to throw in the towel on a writing career, and just resign to pursue a Ph.D., I did three things. One was deep, meditative prayer. This made me remember God is faithful to bring me through the paths He leads me down. Two was pretty practical: I obsessively listened to interviews of other authors and professional writers who say they felt the exact same way. Lastly, is the odd one: I remembered Einstein's theory of relativity.

Seems odd (and probably nerdy) but hang with me. The theory of relativity states that, essentially, there are literal *ripples* in space and time. Think about that for a moment—*ripples in time and space*. Take a bit to chew on that. Let it sink in as much as your time-and-space-bound brain will allow. What does that mean for scientific research? There are places in this realm in which our measurements (and the means by which we inhabit the universe, such as time and space) no longer exist, or at least they don't mean what we think they mean.*

contemplations of a collegiate christian

Milliseconds? Relative.

A square meter? Debatable.

If this is true, it changes a lot. It means this finite, time-and-space contextualized logic that science relies so heavily on cannot be the answer to our every lingering question, to every silent desire in human hearts. Our logic, reason, and measurement-dependent methods do not even necessarily hold up in other places in the universe, and so it can't all be up to logic. There has to be a place for the "illogical," or better, another set of logic.

So, essentially, science and the physical realm can't be the answer to everything. There has to be something more, and I have a suspicion that's where invisible things like souls, cognition, and thoughts come into play.**

And most importantly, our Creator, the invisible God, who is not bound by time or space.

Since ripples in time and space exist, they are worth considering and exploring. It's worth considering that there's more than the physical (i.e.: the metaphysical, or the spiritual), and that if that's true, these metaphysical things can't be studied by physical means. They must be studied by metaphysical means. Actually, I would argue they are the very most important things since we can never fully understand the physical without first understanding its origin: the metaphysical.***

That's a big deal—and a big reason behind deciding that writing about these types of ideas, identity, purpose, and meaning, was important enough to give my life to. I think the Lord has whispered things into my soul that actually matter just as much—maybe even more—than cognitive psychology, and even if they aren't as respected as a doctoral degree by the world at large, I believe it's worth giving my life to. I think there's something beyond the numbers and the

---

If you have seen the movie Interstellar, *it's based on Einstein's theory of relativity and explores these ideas through narrative.*

** *Those fields which usually study these areas are called "the humanities," with the root word being "human," which makes me wonder whether there's just something intrinsically unique to humans to desire things like art, language, culture, etc.*

*** *Because the Father is metaphysical, and the physical's origin comes from Him.*

measurements, more accurately, I think all of the numbers, measurements, and the science are pointing to a deeper reality.

I am pursuing writing now, and we will see what the Lord does with it. I still have to fight the urge to not try to prove my intelligence to the people I talk to daily (because like many academics, I have an undertone of pride in my knowledge that I must fight daily), but I am so grateful God led me down this path instead of a Ph.D.

As for you science majors, you medical school students, you engineers, please don't take this as me saying you should pursue something more "spiritual" or artsy or something. That's not the point of this chapter. We *need* Christian health care workers, lawyers, scientists, politicians, teachers, etc. Those things are important to society, an important way to care for our aching world, and they are just as spiritual when you invite God into your careers.

The point, instead, is I was searching for the answers (the deep, heart-aching type of answers) in my field, and then, I realized they couldn't be found there and that God was calling me into a different exploration.

If you are tempted for a moment to think that the physical has all the answers, just remember:

There are ripples in time and space.

the radical hello

*"There are no ordinary people. You have
never talked to a mere mortal."*

C.S. Lewis, *The Weight of Glory*

A reality of the modern-day college experience is the quiet classroom. I cannot count how many times I've walked into a full classroom, lab, or lecture room and heard only silence. Anywhere from 10 to 500 students are spread out in a room, about 10 minutes before the professor even walks in, with heads bowed to their laps, fingers clicking, scrolling through the same 150 Instagram posts they've seen all morning, responding to another Snapchat of the floor, waiting to get class over with, so that they can go to lunch and do the same thing all over again. The back row is likely full, so those students can get away with scrolling during class too, since the PowerPoint is online anyway, and "the professor has no idea what they are talking about." Hardly anyone introduces themselves to another student. They awkwardly shuffle to the middle of the row, and a mumbled "excuse me" is the first and only phrase you'll hear until the professor starts class.

If the professor asks the class to work in groups or find a partner, you would think it was third grade all over again, students awkwardly staring at the floor, requiring professors to tell grown adults to look each other in the eyes and introduce themselves, like we don't know how to greet another human.

It's such an odd phenomenon, and as much as I get frustrated with it, it just grieves my heart when I really think about it. I'm constantly told our generation, the generation which is now filling collegiate lecture halls and labs, is the most isolated, loneliest, and most anxious one in history. I don't really have another context for what a "normal" pre-lecture setting is supposed to look like beyond what I see in the movies, but I don't think this should be it. I can feel the tension of loneliness, the emptiness of the scrolling, the desire for a real human connection when I walk in these rooms. I've been the person anxiously scrolling, not wanting to introduce myself, so I know exactly what's going on.

However, there's a pretty easy solution, if someone is willing to do it:

Be the first person to say hello.

It's so simple, yet it seems revolutionary and courageous somehow. It's almost always difficult to be the one to break the silence by introducing yourself, but it is infinitely harder in a quiet lecture room. You feel like the weirdo, the one who is admitting they want more than what the screen is offering them, the one who breaks the social norm. A lot of people can overhear your conversation because no one else is talking…and is the person you are introducing yourself to wondering, "Why is this person talking to me?"

But I'm telling you now, college student, ever since I learned this trick, I've been the person to do it over and over again because it's so worth it.

There are various reactions that occur. Sometimes your social "victim" is all for it, and you talk until the professor tells you to quiet down. Sometimes, they are really shy, and you end up asking all the questions, and they don't contribute much beyond a few answers. Sometimes, you end up being class buddies. Sometimes, you never see them in class again because they drop the class.

But somehow, I always know that after I've done it, the human connection was better than the silent isolation.

It might sound silly, and maybe you think I'm a bit dramatic about it, but I really believe it's one of the best acts of kindness you can offer to your college neighbor, and as Christian college students, I hope we are the first to offer this kindness. I want us to stop ignoring our neighbors in preference of our phones, just trying to fit in and get through the course, and start being the ones to say "hello." I want us to be the ones who introduce ourselves, to say hello, to greet the lonely, to invite them into human connection. We all are craving this because we need it. So at least offer it.

I live with a cleaner conscience when I do this, knowing I at least made the effort. Maybe they were too stubborn or prideful or they didn't really want the conversation at all. But I made the offer to a possibly lonely soul.

Start today and make a habit of it now. Start the first week of class if you can, and you will be so grateful in a semester's time that you did this. It is so important, this moment.

We can post about being aware of loneliness, isolation, anxiety, and depression through our screens all day, but unless we take tangible actions towards human connection, I don't think awareness will do a ton. We need more than right belief about this atrocity of loneliness; we need right action.

And this is one of the tiny, baby first steps that make a difference for you and for your college community.

Do you know what's amazing and scary? God created humans out of dust and into flesh and blood, in an instant. We are the most God-saturated invention of all, skin and bones. Humans are His greatest image-bearers. Tears and sweat and beating hearts and souls all mixed up into one package. No one can recreate us in our fullness, consciousness and soul and body and emotion, no matter how hard they try. There's no formula for consciousness that we can come up with from scratch. Two ingredients, sperm and egg, are the only way to create human consciousness.

We are miracles with two legs and arms. We come with personalities and novelties and gender and histories and scars and stories and wrinkles and hurts. We are so *interesting*, the way our brains make connections and adapt, the fact that we *think*, period. The fact that we have personalities and gifts and talents. We are seven billion little miracles on this Earth, each intentionally designed by the Creator, formed in His own image, and made with a purpose.

And yet, we are guilty of trading each other, God's holy invention of humanity—the crowning glory of creation, the image of *Himself*—for ten minutes some electric photons, a digital image, and pride. Something that isn't beating or hurting or longing for more.

We like the images on the screen and the media outlets more than people because they are *easier* to like. Images and media show what you want to see, and people are messy and struggling, convicting and uncomfortable at times. *I* am messy and uncomfortable at times. Humans aren't the same in real life as they are in Hollywood and Instagram.

As the Isrealities did, we make God, and certainly His creation, into our own image. We just do it through the screen now. We make ourselves into what *we* define as worthy. It's different for everyone, our definition. But it is often this: perfect skin, hair, angles, just the right amount of "authenticity," our highlight "real," in just the way that we deem it acceptable.

Our gods are the ones we can control and define, the gods that are in our pockets and hands. These gods aren't so risky as the Sovereign One who asks us to do hard things like acknowledge and speak dignity to His image-bearers. Our gods are something manageable and at our fingertips, in the most literal sense, and doing real life with the people in our physical space is too *risky*.

But I want us to look a little longer and dig a little deeper into humanity around us. Look at the faces of the people you are around. Ask harder questions of your classmates. Be curious about the jobless woman on your bus. Start examining all the assumptions you've had about the people you see in your everyday life.

I think we will find that there's more to God's crowning glory, to *real* humanity than highlight reels. Right here and right now, flesh and blood, skin and bone, tears and sweat, are more satisfying and real than a toxic relationship with the screen could ever be.

The other month I learned that my bus driver Miss Renee has one daughter who goes to my university, and we actually took the same class. Miss Renee loves crime shows, and she wakes up at 4:15 most mornings to come to take me to school. She loves a good barbeque. We talk every day on the bus now.

The other week I sat by a man at my brother's high school graduation. I had left my phone at home and initiated some conversation. When he found out I was a psychology major, he told me that he had PTSD from which he still hasn't healed. I told him he needed to get counseling and that God is a healer. He was so thankful, and I gave him the number of a local pastor.

I will remember Miss Renee forever. I will remember her laugh and the stories she told me about her daughter. I will remember that man forever, and today, I pray he knows the Lord as Healer better today than he did that hot day in May when we sat by each other at a graduation ceremony.

Those moments on the bus to school, at my brother's high school graduation, could have been different if I'd decided to stare at my phone and not make eye contact with that man or Miss Renee. Maybe those conversations didn't seem life-changing at first, and they were even just a bit awkward (as these things usually are.) But dialogue acknowledges each other as human and it's dignifying because exchanging words with someone is a testament to the fact that people are worth more than Instagram or Netflix. Face-to-face human interaction honors one another as humans. It's truly a priceless gift.

How many Miss Renee's have we missed, friends? How many people who are hurting and just need to see another human's eyes, just need a little smile and conversation? We are missing people. Trading our families for Candy Crush, genuinely shared experiences that erupt into laughter for direct-messaging memes.

As C.S. Lewis said, we never interact with mere mortals. We are all immortal—either on the way to death or to life.

So whoever you sit by today in class, whoever you talk with at the lunch table, whoever you possibly ignore in the hallways* —they are eternal beings in need of love and Jesus.

That's worth considering, I think.

I want to make my pre-lecture sitting time count for eternity's sake. I want my five-minute breaks to dignify His crowning glory of creation. I want to testify to the lonely student with no chemistry lab partner that they are worth more than whatever is on social media that day.

---

* *I'm not saying you literally just walk down the hallways and greet every single person. There are definitely days when we are just too tired and need a moment or, perhaps, have been talking too much all day. And sometimes, we legitimately need to look at our phones. There's personal wisdom for each and every situation. Sometimes, you just need to answer that text. Not trying to be legalistic about conversing with people, but I do want us to consider that face-to-face conversation and eye contact speak volumes to a world desperate for hope.*

Hello's might not be *easy*, but they're glorifying, and that's worth something eternal.

TWENTY FIVE

searching for approval

For am I now seeking the approval of man, or of God? Or am I trying to please man? If I were still trying to please man, I would not be a servant of Christ.

The Apostle Paul, Galatians 1:10, ESV

It seems that a theme of adulthood is making very formative decisions about life. Things like where you move, where you go to college, what you major in, what career path you choose, who you date and marry, how you date and what your marriage looks like, how many children you have, how to educate those children, and the list doesn't end. The major decisions are never-ending.

I'm learning that no matter how many hours in prayer, no matter how much wisdom you seek, and no matter how sure you are that's where the Lord is calling you, we will all make many decisions in our adult lives that people just don't like. This is not a matter of if someone frowns on your decision... it's when. And when it happens, their disapproval will likely be clear, whether they realize it or not, and even whether they *want* to show it or not. They might show forthrightly how much they disapprove, by verbalizing their opposing opinion of your life choices. Or, even though they might try to hide their disapproval and frowns, it will still be made obvious by their forced smiles. The person might not even mean to be discouraging, but they don't possess the ability to hide their reactions.

I'm also learning that, no matter how much you think you don't care about their opinion, you will care at least a little at times. Take it from me, the queen of ignoring other people's opinions and thoughts. I am naturally stubborn and independent, and the people who I'm closest to would definitely say I'm *not* a people-pleaser—at all. I can actually be the opposite of a people-pleaser, playing the devil's advocate just for the fun of it. I don't shy away from confrontation, even when I probably need to. (I'm working on this.) But no matter how much I act like I don't care about others' opinions, and no matter the front I put on, at the end of the day, if I'm being honest, I want people to like my decisions.

I know I'm not alone in this; I don't know anyone who has fully conquered the fear of man yet. The only people I suspect may have are old, wise, wrinkly people who have walked through enough seasons of fearing man to know it isn't worth it.

So, how does this fear of man expose itself? You might choose to hide part of the truth in order to avoid a disapproving stare. You might change your phrasing about your career to make it sound more appealing like you're doing a round-about sales pitch. You will secretly hope, in your heart, this person will give you an approving nod, for once. You will pray they will just affirm you, maybe just for a moment. You want to feel supported in your convictions, just this time. When people don't like your choices, either showing it forthrightly or subtly, you find yourself being defensive, trying to hide that you are breaking just a little inside.

You—however subtly—crave their approval.

And, if you're like me, you will probably be surprised at yourself when you look up and you're crying big, toddler-like tears over someone's opinion that shouldn't matter to you so much, like the random stranger at a dinner party who made a slyly degrading comment about your life choices. You tell yourself she has terrible fashion sense and hasn't worked a day in her entire life anyway—but you're still the one who's crying. And you wonder to yourself why in the world you're crying so much because you didn't realize how much you cared about what others thought of you until the moment you were staring at yourself in the bathroom mirror, throat tight, tears falling onto your cheeks.

These moments happened a lot during college, and so I decided to dig deeper into them, to get to the bottom of why I found myself defensive at the slightest hint of disapproval. Why was I hurting so much over this? Was I really that insecure about my life choices? Didn't I know God called me to this?

My issue was not that I craved approval—humans were made for that. It was that I valued human approval over God's approval, or, at least, I valued them both equally. I valued the smiling nod of a random stranger at the dinner party more than the favor of an Almighty King. I put more weight on "That's great, you will make a lot of money and be comfortable, and I think you should do that!" from a human rather than a "Well done, good and faithful servant," from my Lord.

I had focused so much on gaining the approval of the world, so much time and energy, that I had forgotten the eternal, unchangeable approval that is available in my King.

Seeking approval was not the issue. In fact, this search was inevitable. We were meant to be loved, honored, and cherished. My issue was *where* I was seeking approval.

My issue was not my search for approval, but the origin of the approval. Human praise (of my professors, my family, my friends, the random stranger at the dinner party, etc.) had taken the throne over my true King's praise. And so, when what I valued the most wasn't given to me, I panicked. What I'm realizing is that I wouldn't have panicked so much if I'd valued God's approval because I had it already.

The most evident way this surfaced in college was in discussing career and education beyond a bachelor's degree. For those of us who aren't headed to excessively monetary valued careers, we often receive disapproval, or at least the absence of encouragement, when we reveal our career paths.

For me, the conversation usually played out similar to this:

"So, what are you majoring in?"

"I'm a psychology major!"

"Oh, so what do you do with a psychology degree? You're going to graduate school, right?"

"Well a lot of psychology majors do that, but I love to write, and I've been working for the college newspaper and even won some awards! And I'm actually writing a book right now, so I'm just seeing where the Lord leads this skill

and passion that He's given me."

"Oh, okay...Well, that's cool. Maybe you could work at writing for a law firm or a medical clinic! They make a lot of money, you know."

"I'm willing to work whatever job I can get right now, for sure, so I might look into that. Down the line, though, I'm actually hoping to find a job where I write about either culture or Christianity or maybe both."

"Oh, that's nice. Well, I hope that works out and you find a job."

(What am I supposed to say to that? *"Me too"*?)

Awkward silence. End conversation.

In the past, I left these conversations feeling disappointed in myself because I felt like a disappointment to them. Their words would nag and tease my soul for the rest of the evening, eating away at the hope of my career calling, until I went to bed. And before I laid my head down, I would pray that somewhere out in the job market, someone would need a writer for something—anything. I would pray I wasn't worthless and that my work and my writing might matter, somehow, to someone, any human, anywhere. I would pray there was a place in the job field, at least in some small part, for people like me. I pray, somehow, I didn't misunderstand my giftings. I go to bed feeling worthless, a little strung out, a little low on hope, a little misunderstood, and very low on approval.

So, I re-evaluated my heart towards God because this area of my life had been out of line with Him for a while now. I eventually found a rhythm that re-aligns my heart when I start to fear man.

It starts with this: I get down on the hardwood floor of my bedroom and confess to the Lord that I have belittled His glorious opinion. I have put more weight on the temporary and shifting opinions of the world and exchanged His eternal approval for a fleeting one. I confess this sin and ask Him for forgiveness and newness of heart. I know He will meet me here on my knees, in my humiliation, because He always does. He's both a benevolent King, demanding righteous-ness and a kind Father, kneeling down to lift up my face, offering forgiveness.

After I do that, I look up passages that relate in Scripture. I know there are verses, like Galatians 1:10 and the parable of the talents. I study those in the Old Testament who feared God the most, who valued God's approval the most, like Noah, Abraham, and David. Then, in the New Testament, Joseph, who married a pregnant teenager, Joseph of Arimathea who buried the bloody Jewish man who claimed to be the Messiah, and Paul, who "counted everything as loss" except to know Christ (Philippians 3:8).

Then, I ponder Him and His righteousness and goodness, *why* His opinion matters so much more than humanity's, even wise Christian opinions. I reminded myself of this: *He* is worthy. He *is* worthy. He is *worthy*. No one else. No human compares.

Then, I worship Him for His worthiness. His goodness, righteousness, and kindness will lift my soul high, positioning my heart rightly.

It is vital for college students to start this practice in their specific season because, from my experience, college is just the beginning of disapproval, and I don't want to live my life crying over the lady at the dinner party. I want to live my life with hands lifted to the One who looks on me with delight. I want to live my life dancing in the joy of His approval. I want "well done, good and faithful servant" to be my goal, not the fleeting adoration of man.

After this confession and repentance, my attitude toward the disapproving stares changes. They don't hold so much weight, and I am actually able to respond more kindly to myself and to the random person who I just met because they aren't withholding the approval I need; I already have the approval from the One who is above both of us.

As for the practical side, I also have a new plan for when this pattern tries to repeat itself. When someone gives disapproval, for whatever the situation will be, this is how I will respond:

First, I choose not to be mad at them. It's helpful for no one, and this is a good opportunity to have a conversation about other interesting and wonderful career paths (that aren't medical school and law school), and so, I don't want to ruin it by being irritated. They could have great intentions, and if I'm just being sensitive because of past experiences, I could ruin a good conversation. I choose to let them know why I love what I love and give them the benefit of the doubt that they will talk *with* me about it and not *at* me. I invite them into the excitement of my passion; I let them know what sparks my interests and why I chose my future career. I will choose vulnerability. They might be receptive, and they might not. Either way, I give them every invitation to be kind and understand if they don't understand yet.

Secondly, I make a point, unless they ask me, to not explain why I'm not becoming a doctor or lawyer or something that makes a lot of money. I don't owe anyone that. It's not even helpful, and it should be pretty obvious—God is calling me to something else. I'm not here to state a case for my life choices; I'm simply inviting them into my excitement if they'd like to understand.* If they don't actually want to know about my major and career, I don't have much to offer them in this conversation.

Lastly, I ask them about their career or what they spend their labor on because I'm not the center of the world. Maybe they are a stay-at-home mom; I ask them what they love the most and value the most about it. Maybe they are a banker; I ask them what the most interesting thing they do during the day is, how long they've been working, etc. (I'm still working on questions for bankers. I don't know much about finances.) Maybe they are an insurance agent; what's the craziest incident they've dealt with before? Maybe they are a doctor or lawyer; what is their favorite thing about their work? How has the practice of medicine or law changed over the years? Do they like the changes? What are their hopes for future generations of doctors and lawyers? Maybe they're retired; what did they do? Was their career fulfilling? What was the best decision they made about their career? What do their children do now? There are more jobs and careers than my own; I'm going to remind us both of that.

This last step shows we are both adults and, though I'm new in the career world and adult world, we can learn from each other. This can be a conversation and not a one-way lecture.

At the end of it all, I stop and pray. Ask the Lord for this momentary trust. Trust the prayers I've been praying, the answers He's been giving. Trust the gifts and talents He gave me; trust the gift-giver. Trust the passion and excitement He put in my heart.

---

* And if you are disappointed that I'm not applying, well now is your grand opportunity! I'm not applying to medical or law school, so you have a better chance at getting in! Go ahead and apply yourself! Live out your dreams through your own life!

searching for approval

Then, I remember this: we need writers, authors, illustrators, photographers, musicians, poets, philosophers, chefs, bakers, dancers, painters, art teachers, actors, playwrights, potters, architects, craftsmen, fashion designers, etc. I need them. You need them. Their work matters; your work *matters*.

Writer Shauna Neiquist says it like this,

"I know that life is busy and hard, and that there's crushing pressure to just settle down and get a real job and khaki pants and a haircut. But don't. Please don't. Please keep believing that life can be better, brighter, broader because of the art that you make. Please keep demonstrating the courage that it takes to swim upstream in a world that prefers putting away for retirement to putting pen to paper, that chose practicality over poetry, that values you more for going to the gym than going to the deepest places in your soul. Please keep making art for people like me, people who need the magic and imagination and honesty of great art to make the day-to-day world a little more bearable."

I beg with Shauna to myself and to others who are tempted to give up their artistry for something more traditional and more stable, something less risky: *please don't*. We need the art you make. I need the art you make.

At the end of the day, do you know why art matters? It's not because it's mine or yours, but *because the Lord called you to it*. It is significant because *He* says it is because He thought it was enough to call you to it. He is the source of its value—not me, not your professors, not your parents, not the random advice-givers, not even you.

He is.

And if the God of the universe thinks it's important enough to call you there, it logically must be.

And if His opinion isn't important enough to convince you or anyone else, nothing will ever be.

I'm holding on to this truth: God won't call us to anything less than something eternal, something worthy of His approval. I will answer to Him at the end of my life for how I used the passions and skills He gave me, not to my professors or the grown-ups in my life—and certainly not to the random lady at the dinner party. And my decision to follow His lead now will determine how much my heart will sing in that moment.

Here's to basking in His approval.

TWENTY SIX

the better portion

"Martha, Martha, you are worried about many things, but only one thing is needed. Mary has chosen what is better, and it will not be taken away from her."

Jesus of Nazareth, Luke 10: 41-42, NIV

I am named after Mary of Bethany, the sister of Martha, the little-bit-off-her-rocker Mary in the Bible. The "crazy" Mary who poured her year's salary all over Jesus' feet. The one who held tightly to every word the rabbi said while Martha slaved away in the kitchen. Who was accused of being lazy and unhelpful by her sister. Who used her expensive perfume to lather Jesus's feet, who sobbed all over His big toe, who used the very hairs of her head, her crowning glory, to wash the dirtiest part of His body. The Mary who actually recognized Jesus for all that He was, who gave Him the honor due in His presence.

My mother named me this because she often identified with Martha more than she would like. Martha, with her busy, wrung-out, too-tired-to-really-listen-to-Jesus spirit. Martha with her need to prove her desire to earn. Martha with her misunderstanding, divided heart. Martha, who didn't recognize the guest in her home for who He was—the God of the universe.

When I first believed that Jesus was the Savior and I was a sinner, Mary was never more fitting. The Holy Spirit's work led me to desire Jesus' feet, to hear Him speak, to recount every utterance of His Life in me, to be baffled by His majesty daily. I loved nothing more than just feeling His presence, just knowing Him more.

In my heart of hearts, I identified more with Mary. I thought Martha was a little bit of a stick-in-the-mud. I mean, come on Martha, just chill and trust Jesus! It can't be *that* hard. Being Mary was more fun, anyway. Why wouldn't someone want to be Mary, sitting at the toes of the Savior of the Universe, at the hem of the deity, this God-man? It was way cooler than washing dishes if you ask me. Frankly, in my book, Martha is a goody-two-shoes, a no-fun impressor, and she was always missing out. She's worn out and probably has to do a lot of dishes because she cooks so much. Mary is exciting and probably dances harder at parties. Mary is more of a hippie. I liked being Mary.

But as I am graduating college and headed into a new season of marriage and full adulthood, I have begun to feel for Martha. I feel the lure of her busyness. I am learning that it grows more enticing with age, more tempting with more responsibility. The more free-reign I get in my life, the more things I am responsible for, the more illusion of control I have, the more I want to check off the to-do list, the more I want to crack down on every seemingly loose end in my life, the more I want to do, do, do and go, go, go. The more I want to say, "Everybody, look what I'm *doing*! Validate me! Tell me that I'm awesome and I'm not a waste of matter," the more, I ashamedly admit, I am tempted to scowl at those who can find time to sit with the Lord for an hour during the day.

The older I get, the more I understand Martha's temptation to check off all the physical work and forget the spiritual work of resting in Jesus's presence.

Mary is a really easy role to play when you're fourteen years old and free of responsibilities. It's not so hard or risky to trust, not so daunting to stop doing.

When you get older and you realize that the trash has to be taken out, that resumes don't build themselves, and money really, actually doesn't grow on trees or sometimes even in jobs for that matter, it's harder to sit down at His feet as much. It's easier to start doing and stop trusting. The labor of Mary seems more like a risk, a burden, than a gift. The labor of Martha becomes more appealing.

And so you do, and you go, and then you see some fruit of your labors. You see the human praise come, the grades rise, the bank account builds.

Martha's reward is really nice for a while, and the fruit of your labor tastes sweet at first. (Because it is good to labor and work! God said so, and I'm sure Mary did her fair share of earthly labor.) Then, you get patted on the back, and you're labeled "responsible" and you don't feel like a burden to people. People say they pray their children will turn out like you, and it feels good for that moment.

But then, the overtime starts to take its toll. You plow a little too long, and your fruit turns a little sour and rotten because you've forgotten to enjoy it for all the work you've been doing. All of the sudden, the trash being taken out and the grades and money and resume become your credibility, your ticket, your salvation, your validation, and they weigh your soul down instead of lifting it up.

Being worn out kind of feels like a trophy of achievement at first, but then it gets pricey. It's become too much, too weighty of a burden to bear, and I haven't found enough validation in this Martha type of work to keep doing it. No one can ever praise me enough to quench my thirst, and I could always be impressing someone else a little more. When I choose Martha, the answer to my hurt is always *more. Do more, go more, push more, get more, earn more.*

One day, in a quiet afternoon at my home, with a heavy heart, I could feel the cadaverous ache forming in my chest. My addiction to busyness bubbled to the surface, my hands and mind searched around for something to accomplish, something to handle, but I came up short, and the silence got a little too loud.

I want to be a Mary again, I thought.

The Martha pattern doesn't come without expense—the expense of sitting at His feet, soaking in His love. The expense of the intimacy my soul was made for. The expense of rest and trust. The expense of missing out on grace and mercy. The expense of missing the point, missing my Savior, missing my portion and my cup—at the expense of *Jesus*.

The Jesus I don't earn. The Jesus I can't work for. The Jesus I can't buy. The Jesus I can't accomplish. The Jesus that saves sinners and not doers.

We get a choice—life or death, sin or holiness, joy or sorrow, grace or slavery, towards God or away from Him.

I get a choice: Martha or Mary. I don't get both.

I feel for Martha, now that I'm older. I identify with Martha more; I ache for her. There are days and times when I might answer to "Martha" faster than

"Mary." I see where she's coming from, and I want to console her heart, tell her Jesus is enough. I want her to know He will take care of it. I want to shout at her, want to whisper through the pages of the Gospel account of Luke, through time itself, hoping she can hear me through all the time and space between us:

Sit, Martha. Turn off the stove, hang up the apron, let dinner be a bit late. Listen, believe, and trust Him.

Sitting with Him is sweeter. Sitting with Him has peace that's ironically Earth-shattering and stage-stopping. Sitting with Him is the better portion.

Responsibilities are real. Money and resumes are real, but we only need to do what God has given us to do. We can't earn Him. We can't woo Him with our works. We can't control or earn something that's a free gift. He's just asking us to trust and labor to glorify Him, not to earn Him.

I know I will stumble into Martha in later seasons. I pray, though, I am too busy looking at Jesus' face, pouring out my perfume at His feet, honoring Him, to give in to the lie of "the more I do, the more I'm worth."

Right now, I'm going to stop scrounging through my planner for something more to do, even after I've checked it all off for the day. I'm going to get up from the desk, grab a pillow, get down on the hardwood floor, and do the sweet labor of trust I've been craving for so long. I'm going to open Scripture, pray to Him, listen to Him, and choose to believe His presence is enough.

He is sweeter.

He is my better portion.

TWENTY SEVEN

just enough

"How much money is enough?"
"Just one more dollar."
J.D. Rockefeller

"Yet true godliness with contentment is itself great wealth.
After all, we brought nothing with us when we came into
the world, and we can't take anything with us when we leave it.
So if we have enough food and clothing, let us be content."
The Apostle Paul, 1 Timothy 6:6-8

College life is notorious for many things—being late, entering class disheveled, experimenting with irresponsibility, putting off studying, and pulling all-nighters.

All of these things can easily be avoided with proper planning and self-control, however, the "broke college life" is virtually unavoidable.

Now, let me be the first to say I am not literally "broke," and I have no experience to identify with impoverished people. However, before college, I had very little idea about what practical things like razors and apples, shampoo, air conditioning, and running water cost. Who knew you had to pay for weird things like textbooks and parking your car? Who knew tithing and taxes pertained to my measly income? Who knew they could add up so quickly?

Even if you call up your parents, knowing they will give you money (with enough sweet-talk), many college students, myself included, have too much pride for that. And many of us honor and recognize our parents have already done more than enough for us already, and we don't want to take advantage of them.

So, while $7.25 an hour seemed like a pretty good deal in high school, I began to realize that it didn't quite foot the bill in my college life, and for a while, the reality of being "college broke" was just something to complain and joke about.

"I need to get shampoo!"

"But not if you want to eat!"

Laughter. Nonchalant jokes sprinkled casual conversations, and passive-aggressive complaints about not being able to afford $30 concert tickets and gas money for the band that was coming to the town two hours down the highway.

However, after a season of prayer about my finances and a grossly candid heart examination, I have come to the conclusion that every one of my complaints and every single thought of "not enough" is a secondary, skewed, and privileged perspective, and primarily, a heart issue.

First, every complaint about my finances is ridiculous because the Lord has been so, so good to me. The fact I even got to go to a college that cost thousands of dollars is honestly incredible. Plus, all of my friends got to go too, and we got to experience this fantastic and radical season of innovation, change, and growing up hand-in-hand. We were becoming adults together. We were growing into ourselves, into maturity, into future marriages and careers and baby bumps and cross-country moves together. It was truly an unimaginable blessing.

Even if I had to leave for financial reasons, God is good, and He provided for a certain amount of years—that's enough to be praise-filled for the rest of my life. And, as an added bonus, He provided enough work, like random babysitting jobs, coffeehouse dates, and gas for day trips enough to make my heart sing. I have a car that takes me places. My friends and I have enough dollars to throw birthday bashes and to cook for one another every now and then. These moments and these opportunities are sheer grace and to give Him anything less than endless praise is an atrocity.

Most importantly, my heart was out of sorts. Essentially, everything comes down to a heart issue, but money is high on the list of topics in the Bible—about its deceit, about its enticing nature, about how God will make our souls overflow with or without it, and how money was never meant to fill the Him-sized void. Joy is independent of money.

When I am tempted to complain or begrudgingly think *"not enough,"* I, honestly, in my heart of hearts, think I am owed something. I think God's providence has not been enough for my total gladness. I think I should have some amount of money to have the (ironically) intangible joy that the Bible talks about. I think it can literally be bought and that my "lack" or minimum wage is what is keeping me from true joy.

When I sober myself to the reality of my sin, when I realize joy can never be found within a salary, that the Gospel cannot be bought, that love is priceless, and that grace and mercy and all the things that set the world into being are free, are mine without money and without cost; when I decide to forgo complaints and put on the "garment of praise"—only then are my eyes lifted from my "lack" to His abundance and providence.

Only then is opening the envelope of my paycheck turned from a dreadful, disappointing moment to an exciting, provisionary experience.

Only then have I found, most ironically, tremendous wealth and overflowing gratitude from my heart—regardless of the wealth or poverty of my bank account.

Only then is my "minimum wage" turned from a *"not enough"* into a satisfying, heart-lifting, *"just enough."*

This "just enough" is surprisingly, magically life-giving. It's sneakily satisfying to be on the edge of daily bread, like when it's the end of the month, and despite your careful planning, your spending money is running low, and you pray to spend wisely enough to buy some turkey and some sandwich bread. And He provides. And what you once viewed as crumbly white wonder bread and cheap deli meat tastes like joy with every bite.

And then, one week, you really need an opportunity to make some cash, and someone texts you about a babysitting gig in the last few days of funds. All of the sudden, babysitting turns from a "have to" into a "get to."

contemplations of a collegiate christian

And He continues, over and over, to provide the heart-attitude and the practical means of "just enough," like a clock going around and around every day and every week and every month and every season, like your personal twenty-first-century manna.

When I come to embrace the reality of *daily* bread, putting on my thrifted shoes is a celestial experience, canned soup tastes similar to a five-star restaurant cuisine, and financial setbacks are only an opportunity to get on my knees, to ask and watch God provide either the practical means or the spiritual means to endure through my lack-all with joy. And minimum wage transforms into living in spiritual abundance.

We do not serve a God who promises monetary riches, and yet, He does promise to provide exactly what we need, our daily bread, our daily *"just enough"*—in all areas, not just finances. He promises we will never truly lack in the things that make this life worth living—simply put, joy and Jesus. He promises every spiritual blessing, contentment and true, soul-touching, feet-tapping, heart-praising, worshipful gratitude included.

My heart overflows in gratitude to the Spirit who has taught me that abundant life honestly has little to nothing to do with my bank account.

Yet, there are still days when the ends don't meet. Even when less-than-enough strikes, it offers my soul a unique chance to experience true, raw, clear, undeserved mercy.

Thank you to every adult who modeled deep gratitude and more-than-generous living. It has convinced my own heart of its discontent, and I am better for it. Thank you for all the tables I waited on who gave me a substantial tip after they learned I was a college student, providing beyond my necessities. Thank you to all the people who paid me more than I deserved, to sit on their couch, read, and watch a baby monitor while their child slept peacefully two rooms over. Thank you for all the thrown-together meals, the house-sitting gigs, the leftovers you sent home with me when you could have used them as an opportunity not to cook, the Sunday brunches at church, the car rides, the babysitting references, and the kindnesses you lathered on me.

God has used you to turn my minimum wage into "just enough," and this tangible grace has manifested into a spiritual feast for my hungry soul.

TWENTY EIGHT

tired of the money talk

"Some people in this world are so poor, all they have is money"
Derrick Bingham

I am going to continue the conversation about money for just a bit longer. Since it's a huge theme in adulthood and the Bible has a lot say and warn us about the acquiring of wealth and desire for money, I thought it helpful to continue a bit more and discuss one more thing about our relationship to our salaries and our stuff:

The conversation about money.

The older you get, the closer you get to graduation, the more people talk about it. Salary comparisons—how little or how great it will be. New cars, health insurance, down payments, "measly (insert a job here)'s salary." The complaints about starting salaries. The jokes about the cost of children. The instance that somehow, someway, we always got the worse end of the deal when it comes to finances.

I'm growing weary of it—the money talk. It's wearing me thin, brewing discontentment, and stealing my gratitude. I don't want to discuss it, at least not like this anymore. I've been involved in it myself, and it just doesn't do much good. I always grow more discontent. I want to stop with the complaints, and even the large amount of jokes, about the money. I don't want to discuss how much other people make, how they spend their salaries, or how to make more.

I want to talk about how to serve God with what I have. I want to believe I'm the most blessed because I'm part of God's kingdom and His heir. I want to discuss how I can love God more and money less, how to be a good steward of the gracious gifts He's given me now.

I want to put this truth into practice, in my thoughts and words and deeds and giving. I want to live the truth that this is my portion, and it is *enough, plenty, abundant*. I want the type of gratitude and contentment that jumps up and down at the providence of starting salaries and measly graduate school living.

I want to know, deep in my soul, that God is so good, and His provision extends beyond what I can fathom.

Don't get me wrong—I know it's unrealistic to never talk about money. And money is not the ultimate enemy here. But I think we've become too lax about our fixation—dare I say—our affection for it. I am deeply convicted of this affection, and today is my day of repentance. I am longing for something new here. I am seeking a new way.

Can you imagine conversations in which we discussed people's passions and abilities, and did not have to mention how much their salary benefits from those? We could actually talk about a doctor and their service and skills rather than their salary. Sounds like a relief to me.

Can you imagine if we were as concerned with serving our neighbor as we were about saving for our next purchase? Can you imagine if everyone stopped comparing and just thanked the Lord for His provision?

I can see it, just barely. I fall so very short of this myself, but I can almost imagine it, and I want it. I thirst for that type of life, that type of living water, free of the love of money, full of the Spirit.

So I've decided on a couple of rules I'm going to do my best to put in place in my own life, to brew a grateful heart and diminish anything less:

1. Though money discussion will come up at times, I will aim to focus conversations on people's talents, gifts, skills, and passions and less on their salaries.

2. I will pray often that God strips me of my love of money and gives me a love of His glory more.

tired of the money talk

I might have to adjust and add some along the way, but I think this will be a good start. I know, above all else, this is a heart attitude, and rules are just for the times when my heart isn't in the proper place, and I'm trying to tune it accordingly. I want to start off my young adult years like this.

Communion with Him forever is our inheritance. I think that's worth discussing, worth investing our thoughts, hearts, and finances in. That's a conversation worth having, one that will leave us full, knowing He is forever more than enough.

TWENTY NINE

sabbathing

"After six 'days' of universe-sculpting work, God rested. And in doing so, He built a rhythm into creation itself. We work for six days, and then we rest for one. And this cadence of work and rest is just as vital to our humanness as food or water or sleep or oxygen. It's mandatory for survival, to say nothing of flourishing. I'm not a machine. I can't work seven days a week. I'm a human. All I can do is work for six days and then rest for one, just like the God whose image I bear."

John Mark Comer, *Garden City*

Sunlight breaks through the crack in black-out curtains in our upstairs window, brightening our slanted, red oak floors and opening my eyelids long before my mid-morning alarm. Last night's rest was no less than glorious, but my body still lays heavy after a long hard week, and the promise of a day of rest lightens my heart. I stretch the full-body, toe-to-finger-tip stretch, yawning and squinting like an infant.

Still a little dazed, my eyes blink in slow motion. I wrap the fuzziest blanket I own—the one that makes me feel like I am wrapped inside of a bear—around my shoulders and carefully tip-toe down our creaky stairs. I know, without any evidence beyond routine, that I am the third person awake. Alli went for a sunrise run, and Kendra is tucked away with a cup of tea, her journal, and a good book. Soon enough, Kelley will do what she does best—love on us with cooking. Sometimes, it's buttery homemade pigs-in-a-blanket, or perhaps she will prepare some chicken casserole for a post-worship meal. Amber and S.B. will make an appearance soon after. For an early hour or two, the aroma of coffee will fill our nostrils, whispers will tickle our ears, and cold bare feet will make their way back and forth from the couch to the coffee pot.

Around ten o'clock, we will pile into two or three cars and head to worship. We all have different parts to play—some of us will lead in the band, others will sing in the choir, a few will teach Sunday School, and plenty will coddle new life in the nursery.

In this moment, my heart sings with the Psalmist of Psalm 92:1-4 (ESV):

It is good to give thanks to the Lord,
to sing praises to your name, O Most High;
to declare your steadfast love in the morning,
and your faithfulness by night,
to the music of the lute and the harp,
to the melody of the lyre.
For you, O Lord, have made me glad by your work;
at the works of your hands I sing for joy.

It is befitting; it is good to praise Him. In the morning, in the evening. In all ways possible, declaration and singing and dancing. With all instruments possible, from the organ to the cajon. My soul will sing, "It is *good* to give Him thanks."

Everyone will linger in the pews after, at least for a little while, to catch up on the latest news in one another's lives, planning early morning coffee dates and promising to stop by and visit later on in the week to see the kids.

After worship, we will head home and individually make lunch to eat together. I will toast bread with pesto and reheat brothy soup for lunch. Today, we don't have lunch guests but many weeks we do. After some sporadic reading, I will walk around our neighborhood and do some stretching on the porch. One of our friends will come over with the intentions of some light reading and tea, but we will end up giggling and chatting about her latest theological epiphany. Come seven-o'clock, many of us will settle on the couch, snuggling up for our new tradition of Sunday evening movies.

This is now the rhythm of my Sundays, but it hasn't always been this way.

College Sundays can be hectic, the-day-before-Monday type of days. They are all too often crammed with homework, meetings, birthday parties, campus ministry meetings, last-minute grocery store trips, and the occasional Netflix episode. I have spent too many Sundays this way.

The problem, I now realize, is the list of "light" errands was allowing my calendar to overwhelm me until my Sabbath was no longer a Sabbath at all—it was just another busy day without technical commitments and typical studying.

Instead, I crammed too many things into one week and never asked myself why I could not say "no" to things on Sundays, why I felt a sense of anxiety if I decided not to study and just worship, just fellowship, just *rest* instead.

Over time, the Lord revealed to me a control-hungry heart was at the core of my Sabbath to-dos. If I was not working, then the world might leave me behind. If I was not contributing, then how would I even reach Monday? Or better, once I reached it, how would I *survive* it?

But I have found Monday will come, whether I do the homework or not, and the sun will still shine, and my to-dos will be finished when the time is right, and God is good on Mondays, just as He is on Sundays. He knows what is best for us, both in the command to work and in the command to rest. He's just as trustworthy on all seven days, and it's about time I start acting like He is.

He is king, and I am His servant. He is on the throne, and I am here, falling at His feet. It's time I attend to that true position.

I don't expect every season will include these types of Sundays, and I don't think that "Sunday" and "Sabbath" are necessarily interchangeable (Romans 14:5-6). Sabbathing is an every-six-day practice, not a day of the week. It looks different for different schedules and families and people.

However, I will always cherish and take with me the simplicity of a Sabbath without interruption of a restless, busy, give-me-work heart.

God knew what He was doing when He commanded rest, a day set apart from the rest. He knows better than you and me, better than our professors and bosses, better than our schedules and calendars. He commands the world to spin, and He commands a day to rest in His providence. He commands that we work in order to enter His rest.

contemplations of a collegiate christian

So then, there remains a Sabbath rest for the people of God, for
whoever has entered God's rest has also rested from his works
as God did from his. Let us therefore strive to enter that rest.
Hebrews 4:9-11a (ESV)

I want to strive my entire life, the entire six days, to enter this type of providential rest.

The Sabbath,
     the holy *gift* of rest.

THIRTY

not superheroes, but saints

When Jesus heard this, he told them, "Healthy people don't need
a doctor—sick people do. I have come to call not those who think
they are righteous, but those who know they are sinners."
Jesus of Nazareth, Mark 2:17, NLT

I grew up in church, and I'm so thankful for that. However, though I eventually realized the Biblical reference "the Church" wasn't talking about a building, but a (or the) community of believers, I didn't always understand what it meant to be part of this community of Christians.

When I was young, I thought the adults in my church were Christian superheroes. I thought they knew their Bibles front to back. In my head, they didn't just have the order of the books memorized, but they had the page number of every book memorized, and they could recite the references to any verse the preacher said within a matter of seconds. They always gave their tithe and even beyond because they didn't struggle with greed and always trusted God with their money. They prayed in complete sentences, without any ummm's or confusion or stumbling because they always knew what they should pray. They were never mad with their wives, husbands, or children, and certainly not with God. They were always smiling and composed and polite. They dotted their i's and crossed their t's. They never questioned whether Jesus loved them, and Jesus loved them because they were so faithful, good, and well-behaved.

I thought they wanted me to grow up to be a Christian superhero too, and I thought Jesus wanted me to be a superhero Christian kid in the meantime. Though I never was, I wanted to be the kid who finished memorizing my Bible verses and catechism before the others. I wanted to have a perfect shiny star streak on my Sunday school attendance. I wanted to color the majestic Jesus with the lambs perfectly in the lines, getting all the hues right by blending my crayons. I wanted to answer all the Bible questions correctly the first time. I thought, to be a good child, was to be the one who always was quiet when they were told to be, who always washed their hands in the bathroom for exactly two-birthday song's worth of time. The one who never got their card pulled and the one who always had perfect grades in class.

Though I so longed to be, I never was these things because my rebellious, restless, and carefree nature often trumped any of these desires to achieve or follow the rules. I thought Jesus was trying to make me into a do-good kid, a cookie-cutter picture, a perfect rule-follower, and an ingenious Bible verse memorizer, but I was never truly up to the task.

Then, I grew up and observed in more depth the people I thought were Christian superheroes. I noticed that some of them lost their temper with their children at times, and I watched as they turned to the table of contents to find the book of Jude instead of immediately flipping to the right page. I listened as they sometimes said "ummm" in their prayers and got lost in thought or even that some of them opened their eyes or slouched during corporate prayer. I heard as they stumbled over hard questions, like "Why do people die?" or "Where do they go?"

Time progressed, and small-town talk made its way into my ears. I heard that so-and-so's dad "cheated" on their mom. (What was that? Did he copy her homework?) And they were getting "divorced" because of it. I watched as older people in my church died, beginning to realize they weren't invincible. I listened as people prayed tear-stained prayers rather than calm-and-collected ones. I found out my parents sometimes messed up, and that they had to say the dreaded five-letter word "sorry" too. I found that sometimes my Sunday School teacher had forgotten the verses that I was to memorize, noting that her memory was fallible as well. I began to realize, slowly but surely, they were not Christian superheroes after all.

No, they weren't Superwomen and Ironmen. They were undeniably, so purely and clearly, *human*. Human in its rawest sense…crying and slouching and temper-losing and confused and stumbling. Also, human in its ugliest sense… self-centered, prideful, and deeply sinful. They weren't the morally perfect beings I'd once thought.

And so I had to restructure this idea: if they weren't always so perfect, why did Jesus love them? Or—what a terrible thought—did He even love them after all?

So, in my early teens, I took a second look at these men and women and their relationship to the God-man called Jesus. What was their relationship if they weren't perfect people and a perfect rule-making God?

Eventually, I found out their relationship was one where the humans brought all the baggage, and Jesus took it and gave them life, just because He wanted to. They brought their temper, adultery, greed, pride, umms and confusion, and hard questions, and He offered them grace, loving them into obedience. They brought their sin and fallen nature, and Jesus gave them life and the ability to trust Him and His commandments.

They were simply sinners, saved by grace, drawn together at the foot of the cross, trying and stumbling into the service of their King. And when they messed up, Jesus' love didn't stop or change. They got forgiveness. They could repent. They weren't hopeless. He didn't expect perfection from them. He actually expected them to sin, and He chose to love them anyway. He was long-suffering with these short-sighted sinners because He cared for them.

Saints were not superheroes; they were humans who believed in a love bigger than their mistakes and the brokenness of this world.

Their relationship wasn't based on rules. It was based on love: God's perfect love for them.

Their relationship was founded on Christ's death for their sin and resurrection into new life.

The basis of their relationship was a cross and an empty grave.

It was big-L Love itself.

And that death, that resurrection, that Love—that's what empowered them. That's how they could bring their baggage and ask the hard questions. That's how they could face their sin and humanness without despairing—because He loves and He lives. They could obey because they trusted their Savior, and they didn't have to hide or cover up when they messed up. They could be safe here, with this Jesus man.

I would often forget this in college, and I think I'll forget it in adulthood too. I often thought God wanted me to graduate in four years with a perfect GPA and resume, a plan to contribute greatly to society, financial stability, more Bible verses memorized, and ready to be the perfect Christian wife and mother and career-woman, having mastered the art of the kitchen and mascara and my own weaknesses.

But that's not what God is calling us to—He's calling us to something more real, something more satisfying, something fit for humanity, something more fit for our souls, something we actually can do: to bring our baggage and broken-ness, our hurt and faltering steps, our tears and sin and exchange it all for grace, laughter, praise, gratitude, and true righteousness.

He is more invested in me walking these years with confidence in Him and not myself, and if that requires me failing a class or facing my sin in very intimate ways, so be it. He is more interested in my sanctification, in my confidence in justification than in my salary or achievement or rule-following.

He's calling us to love the mercy we have received and extend it to others with every opportunity possible. And when we fail? He's calling to receive mercy and grace once again, causing us to fall in love with Him all over again, trust-ing His sacrifice can cover every mess-up and rebellion. This is the essence of sainthood.

This is our calling: not to be cookie-cutter do-gooders but to be lovers of mercy as well as lovers of true righteousness.

As I "adult" and step into a new type of maturity, I want to keep this in mind: I am not a Christian superhero. I am a sinner-turned-saint.

I am actually my most mature when I learn to be like a little child—asking for help with my sin, crawling back to the cross, and crying to Jesus to pick me up again.

My non-superhero story is one of a beautiful, big, kind, gracious, loving God who loved a faltering, but-dust, non-superhero child like me.

THIRTY ONE

leaving it all behind

"Our unknowns are known to God, and
He's not afraid of them, because they're His."
Kelley

It was the first of May, and finals were finally behind us. The week had been busy of course, but by junior year of college, we had mastered the art of not worrying as much as we did when we were freshmen. We had learned God could handle our grades—good reports and bad reports. We just did our part in the labor, and He would fill in our gaps as necessary. Whatever the outcome, we knew it all worked together for our good, somehow, someway.

Some of my roommates had finished their finals earlier that week, however, the last day was still packed for me, so I was the last to arrive for our end-of-the-semester dinner.

Three exams and one sixteen-page newspaper later, my head was still trying to process all that had just happened on the ride home. I almost missed my bus stop, the bus driver calling my name for "Whitfield Street!" For the last time, I walked from the corner bus stop, up to our front yard, past all of our six cars, stepping up to our wooden porch.

Walking toward the door, my eyes were glazed and my head was dazed by a long semester and a longer year. My hand involuntarily froze as I reached for the door handle, the laughter inside the Lighthouse breaking my weary contemplation.

I remember standing there for a second, blinking, trying to figure out what had

contemplations of a collegiate christian

fractured my daze. I backtracked to my previous thoughts, and there it was again: the sound of shrieking laughter, accompanied by clinking plates and a dinging oven timer.

Then, the vibrations of pattering feet.

The mixed aroma of Kelley's baguettes and freshly cut flowers.

The flash of a camera and the sunlight flooding its way through the windows.

This was the moment the countdown began. This was the very last time we would make a meal all together in the Lighthouse. The very last time Kelley would sit at our table as part of our home, as we headed to senior year of college and she headed into her first year of ministry. The last time that would gather six bodies around a table built for four, sipping Moscato that flushed our cheeks and asking someone to pass more of Kelley's hand-churned butter to smooth over her crunchy bread. The last time S.B. would stand on the sofa, camera in hand, as she commanded us to smile, and we pleaded for her to take a selfie or hand over the camera so we could all be in the picture. The last time I would gather wildflowers to place in a mason jar to set on the table. The last time we would reminisce about the million memories He had given us in a short nine months. The last time we would be together as the people we currently were, before the summer had its way with us, three months of change waiting beyond this evening.

I savored this thought outside our door, hand still frozen at the knob, the chaos calling me inside.

I paused for a moment in all my five senses: hear it all, feel it all, see it all, smell it all, taste all of this blessing we call the Lighthouse.

The year had been massively hard for all of us, but we never knew hard could be so sweet. Between extreme amounts of homework, side jobs, newly discovered passions, friendships beyond our home, new romantic relationships with all their befuddlement and excitement, church responsibilities, family relationships and fallouts, and just trying to find time to do regular human things, the days took their toll.

That year held a really cold winter, and I will never forget the bus rides home

184

from campus each evening that season, feeling my cold and hollow bones rock back and forth to the beat of stop signs like a promise, like the pattern of heading *home*. In many ways, this home was warmth and renewal, a place to put down all my guards, a place to sink into my bed, a place to be filled up and pointed back to the Gospel.

When we decided to name it the Lighthouse, we didn't realize the truth that name would hold. On hard, dark days, I walked home to five other girls who were full of empathy, love, and light. They did the same for me, and we did the same for anyone that we could. We attempted to give each other the best gift possible: the tangible reality of a life invaded by the Gospel. We held out this light when everything else felt dark and scary.

I didn't want to let our present reality—this rare and precious way of living—go. I didn't want to let the Lighthouse slip through my feeble fingers. I didn't want to forget this type of living—a life saturated in love and light—in the progression towards adulthood. I didn't want to watch it fade in the midst of senior year, of adulting, of growing up. I didn't want to let insurance and weddings and graduation and real jobs—and all the other things that seem to make other grown-ups let go of a Gospel-centered life and supernatural trust—I didn't want them to get in the way of this type of living, this type of joy. As I paused on our porch, I was trying to exert a power that is only His: to stop time, to save this moment forever.

I knew the evening would be full of cheers and sweet tears but walking through the door also meant the season would come to a halt in just a few hours.

I knew time must do what its definition required: continue.

I think this type of fear overtakes everyone at some point, especially during good, mountain-top seasons. Anxieties overwhelm our souls about what life will look like beyond this moment, what lies beyond college, how we will financially support our ever-approaching adulthood, what will become of our current romances and passions if contentment will still be present beyond this season.

We want to hold on to what seems good, even when it's time to let go and evolve. We don't want to move forward because we don't know what the future holds. We try to refuse maturity and hold on to this moment, but this moment will eventually become the past. It's becoming the past, even now, even as you read these pages.

One second gone. Another coming. Gone again. Time is always pressing on.

During that season, the title "seniors" made us want to pee our pants sometimes, so much so that we deemed it the forbidden word, shushing lips and putting our hands over anyone's mouth who would dare to name such a thing.

We eventually matured, learning time would have its way, and we should put the title on and walk in it for a little bit at least, since it was approaching.

That evening we were juniors, in the morning we were seniors.

Eventually, the title "graduates" replaced "seniors," and "dating" became "engaged" which became "married," and Alli just became "Mom" recently. Eventually, in time, our first names might possibly be replaced by goofy grandparent names like "Poppy" and "Nah-Nah" which have little resemblance to our birth certificate names.

There are so many changes, so many shifting variables, so many unknowns, so many "what-ifs," and sometimes I count these as reasons to be afraid.

However, when it really comes down to it, I know I have absolutely no reason to fear the unknowns. God is good, and He was in control of my season in the Lighthouse, and He's in control of my seasons ahead. As I draw near to Him, He has never left me without joy. He is a kind Father, and He doesn't give snakes when we ask for fish. He is a loving Father, outside of time itself, directing it in a way that is most beneficial for His glory and our good.

A good, good God is my parent, my Father, and I am His daughter. In the same way He has held my past and my senior year, He will hold my post-college years, my changing friendships, my marriage, my future children, my trembling fears, all for His name's sake.

He is what made the Lighthouse worth being a part of.
He is the constant.
He is the Light.

leaving it all behind

I realized this as I placed my hand on the doorknob.

So, bearing that one thing in mind, squeezing it— squeezing *Him*—as tightly as humanly possible, I took my tiny hand, turned the doorknob, and embraced the last evening.

I'm in a good season, and the future seems bright most days.

But on the days where it seems dark and scary or at least unsure, I know that no matter the season,

He is my true and better Lighthouse.

acknowledgements

If writing is uncomfortable, then sharing first-drafts is terrifying. I would like to extend my greatest gratitude to Bailey Archey, Rakin Hunter, and Hannah Blakenship, who—when they could have been doing a million other things to improve upon their own accomplishments and dreams—went above and beyond in offering encouragement and kindly editing some of the roughest bits of my rough drafts. They believe in me, and they believe in this book, and that alone makes me want to weep tears of gratitude.

I'd also like to thank other members of my launch team, including Shelby Irby, Madison Weeks, Taylor Walding, Olivia Robbins, Abigail Krutz, Emory Bradford, Madeline Houston, Bronwyn Frost, Nate Freeman, Emma Nimnicht, and Sara Parks Martin, who put up with endless emails which often contradicted one another, and cheered this project on just the same.

Publishing is no easy feat, emotionally or logistically. I'd like to give a special thank you to my publishing team at United House Publishing, specifically Taylor Phillips and Jessica Russell, for allowing me creative freedom and answering my constant (probably somewhat annoying) emails. Your kindness did not go unnoticed.

Thank you, Kyle, for dealing with a million tears and seasons of frustration with my writing. I have never doubted that you believe in this.

Lastly, to my sweetest Lighthouse ladies, and to Sarah Morgan and Mollie: You give me laughter and prayer when I need them most, and this book wouldn't have half its spunk without you. Your existence makes me want to write.

notes

Letter Bible Institute. April 20, 2021. https://www.blueletterbible.org/Comm/hocking_david/attributes/attributes14.cfm

Ackerman, Diane. One Hundred Names for Love: A Memoir. New York City, New York: W&W Norton & Company, Inc., 2011.

Adams, Thomas. The Works of Thomas Adams: Being the Sum of His Sermons, Meditations, and Other Divine and Moral Discourses; Volume 1. Wentworth Press, 2016.

Austen, Jane. Pride and Predjudice. Garden City, New York: Millennium Publications, 1813.

Bingham, Derrick. A Voice Full of Money: The Parable of "The Great Gatsby": A Warning Against Moral Drift. Greenville, South Carolina: Ambassador-Emerald International, 2001.

Chandler, Matt. Recovering Redemption. Nashville, Tennessee: B&H Publishing Group, 2014.

Comer, John Mark. Garden City: Work, Rest, and the Art of Being Human. Grand Rapids, Michigan: Zondervan. 2015.

Cowper, William. "Heal Us, Emmanuel, Hear Our Prayer," Olney Hymns Book i., No. 14, 1779.

Darwin, Charles. The Autobiography of Charles Darwin, 1809-1882. London: Collins, 1958.

Hocking, David. "The Patience of God." The Blue Letter Bible. The Blue

Letter Bible Institute. April 20, 2021. htttps://www.blueletterbible.org/Comm/
hocking_david/attributes/attributes14.cfm

Lewis, C.S. Letters to an American Lady. Grand Rapids, MI/Cambridge, United Kingdom: William B. Eerdmanns Publishing Company, 1967.

Lewis, C.S. Letters to Malcom, Chiefly on Prayer. New York City, New York: HarperCollins Publishers, 1964.

Lewis, C.S. The Four Loves. New York City, New York: HarperCollins Publishers, 1960.

Lewis, C.S. The Weight of Glory. New York: HarperCollins, 1949.

Niequist, Shauna. Cold Tangerines: Celebrating the Extraordinary Nature of Everyday Life. Grand Rapids, Michigan: Zondervan, 2007.

Rilke, Rainer Maria. Letters to a Young Poet. New York City, New York: W. W. Norton & Company, Inc., 1934.

Stieg, Cory. 2019. "Half of Millennials and 75% of Gen-Zers Have Left Jobs for Mental Health Reasons." CNBC. Constumer News and Business Channel. November 22, 2019. http://www.cnbc.com/2019/10/08/millennials-gen-z-have-quit-jobs-due-to-mental-health-issues-survey.html.

Tolkien, J. R. R. The Hobbit, or There and Back Again.. London, England: HarperCollins, 1937.

Vanauken, Sheldon. A Severe Mercy. New York City, New York: HarperCollins Publishers, 1977.

Weber, Carolyn. Surprised by Oxford. Nashville, Tennessee: Thomas Nelson, 2011.

Wilkin, Jen. "Beware of the Instagram Bible." The Gospel Coalition. January 2, 2017. https://www.thegospelcoalition.org/article/beware-instagram-bible/

about the author

Mary Madeline Schumpert (MM) is a new adult, a follower of Christ, and a lover of all things word-related. Mary Madeline longs to see young Christians live authentic and unified in an image-obsessed and polarized culture. She aims for the kindness of grace and the beauty of truth in all that she does. In her free time, she enjoys experimenting with gluten-free baking and watching (and re-watching) her favorite artists' interviews on Youtube. The recent college graduate is an author, writer, and podcaster.

To find more of her work, visit...

earthtomm.com

Follow her on...

Instagram: @earthtomm

Twitter: @merrymadmen.

The Lighthouse, from top left to bottom right:
Sara Beth, Kendra, Kelly, Amber, Alli, and Mary Mad